Contemporary Architect's Concept Series 28

柄沢祐輔 ｜ アルゴリズムによるネットワーク型の建築をめざして

Yuusuke Karasawa | Toward Network Type Architecture by Algorithmic Method

LIXIL出版

Contemporary Architect's Concept Series 28
Yuusuke Karasawa | Toward Network Type Architecture by Algorithmic Method

First published in Japan on January 25, 2021, by LIXIL Publishing

LIXIL Publishing
2-1-1 Ohjima, Koto-ku, Tokyo, 136-8535, Japan
TEL: +81 (0)3 3638 8021   FAX: +81 (0)3 3638 8022
www.livingculture.lixil.com/en/publish

Author: Yuusuke Karasawa
Publisher: Jin Song Montesano
Editor: Shinya Takagi (frick studio)
Text Translation: Atsuko Imaizumi (p022-025), Fraze Craze Inc.(p004-008, p026-161 explanations)
Design: Minori Asada (MATCH and Company Co., Ltd.)
Cooperation: Yoko Taguchi
Printing: Kato Bunmeisha Co., Ltd.

# 目次 Contents

# 脳に反して思考する：
## アルゴリズム空間のパフォーマンス
### エリー・デューリング

過去30年に及ぶアルゴリズムデザインの徹底的な研究、実験を経て、建築理論は分岐点に直面している。一方で、パラメトリック技術の濫用が連続性への執拗な追求と相まって、滑らかな生物形態や質感を財産として手に入れるとともに、装飾芸術への関心の再燃をもたらしている。この新しいマニエリスムは、未だスタイリッシュな雑誌やカタログ、時に私たちの街の風景に大きく取り上げられている。私たちが取り扱う形が歪んだり、折り畳まれたり、または「力場（フォースフィールド）」によって変形したとしても、結果として現れる視覚的スタイルは比類なく連続している。例えシームレスな曲線形状でなく、絡み合わせたり、途切れたり、フラクタルなモチーフに発展したとしても、「連続性」はより根源的、抽象的な次元で（絶えず）作用している。背後に潜む幾何学がどれ程素晴らしく、また「仮想」や「発生」などの概念をどれ程アピールしても、デザインの直観的な即時性に勝ることはない。形態は、連続的または断続的に変形させられた多様体への恒常的な依存によって定義される。マリオ・カルポの観察によれば、この事実はむしろ逆説的な状況を図示している。徹底的にデジタル——つまり基本的に離散的な技術を利用しながらも、建築家のほとんどがコンピューターを決してコンピューテーショナルではない方法で利用している。そうすることで彼らはこの飛躍的に自動化された社会の日常を定義づける一つの要素とのより直接的な衝突を避けようとしているのである[*1]。

一方で、近年のデジタルアーキテクチャは、その計算的な本質をより毅然とした方法で認め、概念や設計に「細かい」計算的技術とアルゴリズムを利用するだけではなく、潜在的に重要な社会的意義を持った新しい生産プロセスによる物理的な建物の組み立てに活用することで、離散性の概念を強調していくべきと訴える声も聞かれる[*2]。あたかもビデオゲームの「マインクラフト」のように、拡張可能な材料部品のモジュール組み立てが多方向に分配されたデジタルデータの工作を映し出している一方で、グリッドストラクチャー、ブロックや「ボックス」を整列したり、クラスターやクラウドに形成するなどの基本的な材料やツールを使用することで、根元的な連続性と機械的なプロセスの美学の提案がある。しかし、これはまた異なる矛盾を引き起こす。それはまるで、離散的な建築の自由なパフォーマンスが、最終的に独自の固定的な視覚的スタイルに堕していくかのようである。その点、「第二のデジタル化」は、良くも悪くもデジタル媒体の裏に潜んだ自然（あたかもピクセル化されたイメージのように単位が反復する自然のモチーフと詩的なアナロジーを取り結ぶことによりそれは達成される）の「粗い」対照物を提供しなければならない。

こうして、デジタルアーキテクチャは柄沢祐輔氏の離散的アルゴリズムデザインとの関わりの中心にある、より根本的な問題をかわしつつ二極の方法で問題系を反復することに終始するだろう。その

根本的な問題はスタイルやテクノロジーを超えた、視覚的思考の徹底的な離散化によって引き起こされる、建築的*体験*の語用論についての領域に達する。これは動作と視覚、または動作の中の視覚によって現象学的に説明することが最善である。なお、効果的に提示するためには、まず初めに具体的な建築的体験を形式化する必要があり、その過程にはある一定の抽象化を必要とする。このモノグラフに配置されている「ネットワーク図」によって鮮明に図示されるに従い、柄沢氏の発明方法は空間構造の下に潜む特定の*トポロジー*に大きな注意を向けさせる。それは連続と断絶、接続と分離の間の交錯のモードについて問うことに関係する。

そのような形態的関係性について例示する方法は多くあるものの、知覚できる建築の範囲においては視覚的距離については分離を、また動的近接（私たちの視界のある要素が「手の届く範囲内」にあると瞬間的に感じる感覚）については接続を思考することが自然である。もちろん、遠位と近位、視覚的と動的は程度の問題として連続的な言葉と理解することができる。ゲシュタルト心理学によって掘り下げられた知覚の法則（例として、図地反転の裏に潜む知覚の法則）は概して局所的な一連の行動の原則に従う平衡化のメカニズムに究極的には依存する。そういう意味では、「遠くの行動」は存在せず、遠位とはただ異なる、または遅れてくる近位の体験となる。しかし、空間的*性質*を構成する限りにおいては、程度の

差異より性質の差異の方がより著しい。すなわち、最初に近位と遠位の分離がある上で、接続と分離の関係が空間の基本的な区切りや性質を明らかにする限り、出現する形態は本質的に離散的である。実際は、そのような関係性に基づき、空間自体が、結局のところすべてを包み込む媒体（均質または不均質に関わらず）ではなく、結節点のネットワークとなる。同様に、特定の観点では*場所*と定義することができる結節点は、絶対的空間における位置として特徴付けられる必要はない。結節点は自身を支える分離的、接続的関係性において、関係的な方法で統合的に定義することもできる。

それらを形式化するために建築的体験の基本となる視覚的、動的な座標に再注目することによって、柄沢氏のプロジェクトは建築を設計、建設するだけでなく、その中で生活する際に、結局のところ最も重大な問題に対して明白な表現を与えることを成し遂げている。すなわち、私たちの脳は、なぜか連続する形態に固執し、結果としてアルゴリズムの過程における離散的な論理や、離散的な空間の未知の領域の本質に適応することが困難だという事実である。

———

脳に反して思考することは、何よりもまず、射影空間の呪文を解く、またはその内側から破壊することである。離散性に対する期待は、射影空間の*内側*に

見つけることができる。日本の伝統的な木版印刷や現代建築図面でよく見られるアクソノメトリック表現技法は、その代表例である。そこでは、浮遊する視点が何かと不規則に二つの相対的に互換性のない視点の間を平行移動し、多安定的な透視画の構成と唐突な図地反転を許容しながらも、絵画空間の奥行き方向の連続的な拡張の錯覚を破壊する。一方アルベルティ的透視画法による表現では、遠位と近位の間に存在する全体的な連続性の感覚は水平線へ収束していく視線を辿ることへの可能性の結果、または視覚的に収斂する事実と徐々に後退する形のオーバーレイ（重ね置き）による手掛かりに依存することである。対照的に、水平線が欠落している、または倍増している場合、空間全体が中断され、幾分不連続である。二つの異なる軸に規定され、それは本質的にせん断しているように見える。

　上記とは幾分異なるものの、その間接的な体験は三次元映像といくつかの建築物によって体験することができる。桂離宮とその周辺の庭園での体験は、建築の構成の可能性について非常に貴重な例を示す。書院と庭園をつなぐ小径を散策すると、それぞれ切り離された風景を周遊する視点が、自身の動作によって再構成するという、特有の動的性質を体験できる。植物や建築の要素は表面上切り取られ、透明な平面に貼り付けられ、お互いに覆い被さりながら、まるでアニメーション動画のために描かれたように見える。変動する光と影の移ろいが混じり合った混合体を引き立てるために通常の遠近の配置をぼやかすことで、庭園は即時に広々として平面的、かつコンパクトで不思議なほど無形的になり、見る者が中心性の感覚を取り戻したり、調整しようとするにつれて、視差移動の絶え間ない相互作用が行われる。人工的にアニメーション化された、自然の変化する風景によって伝達される全体的な印象、また矛盾する視覚的、動的な合図の満ち引きにより引き起こされる視点の一定の置換は、体外離脱体験による無重力状態、または無重力状態での飛行の感覚に類似している。それはまさしく自身が*遠くから没入している*、いわば即時的に接続し切断するような超現実的な質の立体映像に非常に近い。書院建築については、その雁行配置が「シフトする平面の積層」を好み、「すべての対称性や中心性を放棄する」方法として磯崎新によって適切に説明されている。これらは「人間の視点を中心として空間の奥行きを無限の彼方に向かって先導する、西洋の遠近法とは際立って対照的に、奥行きを表現する*3」ように配置されている。内部はある基本的な要素をモジュール化して繰り返すことで発生する移り変わる空間であり、多様なデザインパネルと連結する仮想ボリュームの積層によって偶発的に不透明化されている。ヴァルター・グロピウスによると、「平面には静的な概念、対称性、中心的な焦点がない。ここでは芸術創造の唯一の媒体である空間が、魔法のように浮遊している

ように見える。*4」。その体験は、より形式的なレベルにおいて、離宮の全体的な地形の中で、これらの領域それぞれが他の領域と関わる相対的なアクセシビリティと不可視性の交錯する関係性によって強化される。

———

空間は浮遊している。空間の中の何かではなく、空間自体が、である。流れているのではなく、浮遊している。柄沢氏の《villa kanousan》は、その独特な方法でこのジェネリックな状況の3D投影を提示している。ここでは、「浮遊する空間」はアルゴリズムによって活発な変容の形をとる。その仮想キューブが15度回転し、壁や床、天井を横切るにつれて、その断続的な位置は次第に空間にストラクチャーを与える。そのアルゴリズムの形態形成力は明らかであり、内包された空間を時空間の中にあるその周囲（自然や光）に対して開くことで実際に追体験することができる。
　《s-house》では、アルゴリズムをそのコンピューテーショナル、または装飾的な機能を超えて実生活における空間体験の方向に一歩踏み込んでいる。それは透明性の原則と分離の原則、二つの区別できる原則を結合、実行する。透明性の原則は、住宅の複雑なストラクチャーの中に最大限の視界を開くことを暗示し、私たちがどこに立とうとも、複雑に絡みあう階層が許容する範囲内で、他の多くの場所と視覚的につなぐ

視線を描くことができるはずである。分離の原則は視覚的空間と感覚運動的空間の間にある裂け目——すなわち、住宅内において訪問者の現実的または仮想的な運動に関わる空間である——を認識させる。建築家の分かりやすい説明の如く、ある場所とある場所をつなぐ道は、現実では視覚のみでは知覚できないほど長く、遠回りしている。そこには予期しない迂回路や近道が存在し、私たちはそれらの漠然とした印象しか手足で感じとることができない。対照的に、私たちの目はより速く、また本質的に落ち着きがない。それはほとんど瞬間的に自身から少し離れた仮想的な繋がりのネットワークで囲ってしまう。この違和感は、バイロケーション（一身二箇所存在）、つまり思考と身体の擬似分離という不思議な感覚を誘発する。この場合においては、アルゴリズムデザインは、二つのバラバラな「知覚した」空間の並列処理によって引き起こされる、絶え間ないフェーズシフトの精度の高い重合と分節を達成する。
　透明性の原則と相まって、分離の原則は、視点が奥行き方向に連続的に拡張することを防ぐために一定の不安定性を維持し、一つの単一化された建築的空間の感覚をその特有の離散的変形の集合によって相殺する。この解消されることのない緊張は、コーリン・ロウとロバート・スラツキーの有名な文章への賛辞を込めて、柄沢氏に「虚の不透明性（もしくは虚の曖昧性）」と呼ばれている。この不透明化という概念は、もちろ

ん槇文彦が東京のある道に対して平面の積層と小さな窪みの蓄積が、次第にその場所に奥行きと親密性を形成していくことを説明する時に用いた「奥」という概念に類似している。《s-house》のアルゴリズムによる区切りと間隔の設け方は、透明性と同時性の要素に類似するものを達成する。具現化された視点によって実行される場合、そのバラバラで不連続なストラクチャーは、奇妙に包まれる特質を獲得する。それは私たちを「奥」の秩序と乱雑が繊細に混ざり合った空間によって得られるものに比べ、直接的ではないものの同等の効果のある*形式的親密性*のレベルまで引き上げてくれる。

もし《villa kanousan》が離散的空間の象徴的なエンブレムであるとするならば、《s-house》はその実践的な試験場である。近年のフィリピンの《バンタヤンパークセンター》のプロジェクトにおける渦巻くストラクチャーは、文字通りのネットワークである。ダイアグラムは実寸のスケールまで拡大され、ついに実際の建物と融合し、アルゴリズムの力を完全に解放したのである。

*1  Mario Carpo, *The Second Digital Turn: Design Beyond Intelligence*, MIT Press, 2017.
*2  Gilles Retsin (guest editor), *Discrete: Reappraising the Digital in Architecture*, Wiley, 2019.
*3  Arata Isozaki, *Japan-ness in Architecture*, MIT Press, 2011, p. 273-274 and 286.
*4  Walter Gropius, "Architecture in Japan," in Virginia Ponciroli (ed.), *Katsura Imperial Villa*, Phaidon 2011, p. 355.

エリー・デューリング
哲学者、パリ第 10 大学准教授
1972 年テヘラン生まれ。ソルボンヌ大学、プリンストン大学で学ぶ。2008 年よりパリ第 10 大学准教授。
情報技術が進展を遂げた社会における芸術のあり方を示した
「プロトタイプ」としての芸術概念を提示して、世界的に知られるようになる。

# Thinking against the brain:
# the performance of algorithmic space
# Elie During

After thirty or so years of intensive research and experimentation in algorithmic design, architectural theory finds itself at a crossroads. On the one hand, the abuse of parametric techniques, conjoined with an obsessive focus on continuity, has yielded a wealth of smooth biomorphic shapes and textures, as well as a revival of interest in ornamental art. This new mannerism is still largely on display in stylish magazines and catalogs, and occasionally in our cityscapes. Whether we are dealing with warped and folded surfaces, or objects deformed by "force fields," the resulting visual style is uniquely continuous. Even when it does not translate into seamless, curvilinear forms, developing instead into intertwined, punctured or fractal motives, continuity still operates at a more fundamental, non-representational level. As remarkable as the underlying geometries may be, and despite the appeal of such concepts as "virtual" and "emergence," the intuitive immediacy of *design* prevails. Form is defined by a constant reliance on continuous—or continuously distorted—manifolds. As Mario Carpo observed, this fact illustrates a rather paradoxical situation: while using thoroughly digital—thus basically discrete—technology, most architects are putting computers to service in a way which is anything but computational, thereby avoiding a more direct confrontation with what has become one of the defining features of everyday life in massively automated societies *1.

In more recent years, on the other hand, some have voiced the concern that digital architecture should come to terms with its computational nature in a more resolute way, emphasizing the notion of discreteness not only in the use of "high-resolution" computational techniques and algorithms for conception and design, but also in the physical assembly of buildings according to new production processes with potentially important social implications *2. While the modular assemblage of scalable material parts mirrors the manipulation of versatile and distributed digital data, the use of basic materials and tools such as grid structures, building blocks or "boxes" arranged in rows, clusters and clouds, suggests an aesthetics of raw seriality and machinic process, in the spirit of the video game *Minecraft*. This raises yet another paradox. It is as if the open-ended performance of discrete architecture was bound to yield, in the end, a visual style of its own. In that respect, what the "second digital turn" has to offer is, for better or worse, a "low res" counterpart of the underlying digital medium: a pixelated image bearing new poetic analogies with the ways of nature…

Thus, in two different ways, digital architecture ends up sidestepping the more fundamental issue that I believe is at the heart of Yuusuke Karasawa's involvement with discrete algorithmic design techniques. This issue reaches beyond style or technology; it is about the pragmatics of architectural *experience* induced by a thorough discretization of visual thinking. The best way to spell this out phenomenologically is in terms of motion and vision, or vision in motion. Yet, in order to be addressed effectively, embodied architectural experience must first be formalized, which requires a certain degree of abstraction. As vividly illustrated by the "network diagrams" distributed across this monograph, Karasawa's method of invention crucially turns around a particular *topology* underlying spatial structure. It involves inquiring into the modes of interlacing between continuity and discontinuity, connection and separation.

Now there are many ways in which one may instantiate such topological relations, but as far as the perception of architecture goes, it is most natural to think of separation in terms of visual distance, and of connection in terms of kinesthetic proximity (in the sense where certain elements of our visual field immediately feel "within reach"). Distal and proximal, visual and kinesthetic, can of course be apprehended in continuous terms, as a matter of degree. The laws of perception investigated by Gestalt psychology (such as those behind figure/ground reversals) ultimately rely on mechanisms of equilibrations conforming, by and large, to a principle of local or contiguous action. In that sense, there is no such thing as "action at a distance," and the distal is only differed or delayed proximal experience. However, as far as the constitution of spatial *values* are concerned, differences in nature are more significant than differences in degrees: the disjunction between proximal and distal comes first, and the resulting topology is inherently discrete,

in so far as relations of connection and separation establish a basic punctuation and valuation of space. In fact, based on such relations, space itself turns out to be a network of nodes, rather than an all-embracing medium (whether homogeneous or heterogeneous). The nodes, in turn, may be defined as *loci* for particular points of view, but they need not be characterized as locations in absolute space: they can be integrally defined in a relational manner, in terms of the conjunctive or disjunctive relations that support them.

By refocusing on the basic visual and kinesthetic coordinates of architectural experience in order to formalize them, Karasawa's projects manage to give conspicuous expression to what is, after all, the most pressing problem when it comes not only to designing and building architecture, but living (in) it—namely, the fact that our brains are somehow hard-wired for continuous forms and consequently have a hard time adjusting to the discrete logic of algorithmic process, as well as to the unfamiliar nature of discrete space.

———

Thinking against the brain involves, first and foremost, breaking the spell of projective space—or subverting it from within. Anticipations of discreteness can indeed be found *within* projective space. The axonometric representational techniques favoured by traditional Japanese woodprints as well as by contemporary architectural drawing are a case in point. There, the floating gaze manages to shift, somewhat erratically, between two mutually incompatible point of views, allowing for multi-stable perspectival compositions and abrupt figure/ground reversals, while destroying the illusion of a continuous extension of pictorial space in depth. In the Albertian tradition of perspectival representation, the sense of an overall continuity between distal and proximal results from the possibility to follow lines of sight converging on the horizon, or to rely on cues provided by facts of visual occlusion and the familiar overlay of receding shapes. By contrast, when the horizon is lacking, or when it is doubled, the whole spatial stage is disrupted and somewhat disjointed. Hinging on two different axes, it appears essentially sheared.

A different but related experience is provided by stereoscopy and some of its indirect architectural counterparts. A visit of the Katsura Imperial villa and its surrounding gardens offers an invaluable example of what architectural composition can achieve in that respect. Every visitor who had a chance to stroll along the paths connecting the *shoin* to the garden can attest to the peculiar kinematic quality that results from breaking down the scenery into parts that the touring gaze will reassemble by its own motion. The vegetal and architectural elements are seemingly cut-out and pasted upon transparent planes, overlayed and gliding on each other, as if drawn for an animation movie. Obfuscating the usual distribution of far and near in favour of a fluctuating assemblage of chromatic

intensities, the garden appears at once spacious and flat, compact and strangely incorporeal, allowing for an incessant interplay of parallactic shifts, as one tries to adjust and recover a sense of centeredness. The overall impression conveyed by the changing scenery of this artificially animated nature, the constant displacement of the gaze that is induced by the ebb and flow of contradictory visual and kinesthetic cues, is akin to the sense of weightlessness one may get from an out-of-body experience, or from a flight in zero-gravity. It is, certainly, very close to the hyper-real quality of stereoscopic views in which one finds himself *immersed from a distance*, so to speak, at once connected and disconnected. As for the *shoin* itself, its diagonal arrangement, reminiscent of a "flying geese formation," has been aptly described by Arata Isozaki as a way of "renouncing all symmetry and centrality" in favour of "a layering of shifting planes." These are arranged "to express depth [...] in sharp contrast to Western perspective, which marshalled depth of space toward infinity by taking the human gaze as central [3]". The interior is a mutable space engendered by the modular repetition of certain basic elements, with the occasional opacification produced by the layering of varied design panels and interlocking virtual volumes. In Walter Gropius' words: "No static conception, no symmetry, no central focus in the plan. Space, here the only medium of artistic creation, appears to be magically floating [4]." The experience is intensified, at a more formal level, by the interlocking relations of relative accessibility and invisibility that each of these sectors entertains with the others within the overall topography of the villa.

———

Space is floating. Not something in space, but space itself. Not flowing, but floating. Karasawa's "villa kanousan" offers, in its own way, a 3D projection of this generic situation. Here, the algorithm takes the form of an active transformation: as a virtual cube is rotated by 15 degrees, cutting across the walls, floors and ceilings, its successive positions gradually give structure to space. The morphogenetic power of the algorithm becomes palpable, it can be relived in real time, opening up domestic space to its spatio-temporal surrounding (nature and light).

"s-house" goes one step further in the direction of a real-life spatial experience of the algorithm, beyond its purely computational or ornamental functions. It conjoins and implements two distinct principles: a principle of *transparency* and a principle of *disjunction*. The principle of transparency implies a maximal opening of the visual field within the intricate structure of the house: wherever we stand, we should be able to draw lines of sight that connect us visually with as many other locations as the complex intertwining of levels allows. The principle of disjunction introduces a rift between visual space and sensory-motor space — i.e., the space associated with the real or virtual movements of the visitor inside the house. For reasons that are well explained by the architect, the paths connecting one place to another are in reality longer, more circuitous, than what sight alone may suggest. There are unanticipated detours — as well as shortcuts — of which the foot and the hand only have a vague impression. The eye, by contrast, is much faster, and naturally more impatient; it almost instantaneously surrounds itself with a web of virtual connections at a distance. This discrepancy induces a curious feeling of bi-location, a quasi-dissociation between mind and body. What algorithmic design achieves, in this case, is a precise layering and articulation of the ceaseless phase shifts induced by the parallel processing of two disjointed "felt" spaces.

Coupled with the principle of transparency, the principle of disjunction prevents the gaze from continuously expanding in depth. It maintains a level of instability, which counterbalances the sense of a single unified architectural space, with its distinctive group of discrete transformations. This unresolved tension leads to what Karasawa calls a situation of *phenomenal opacification* (or phenomenal obscuration), as a tribute to a famous text by Colin Rowe and Robert Slutzky. This idea of opacification is of course reminiscent of the concept of *oku*, which has been used by Fumihiko Maki to describe the way the layering of planes and the accumulation of small recesses gradually build up a sense of depth and intimacy in certain streets of Tokyo. The algorithmic punctuation and spacing out of "s-house" achieves something similar in the element of transparency and simultaneity: when performed by the embodied gaze, its disjointed and fractured structure acquires an oddly enveloping quality. It raises us to a level of *formal intimacy* that is less immediate but no less effective than the one obtained by the delicate mixture of order and disorder displayed by *oku* spaces.

If "villa kanousan" is the prismatic emblem of discrete space, "s-house" is its performative testing ground. As for the swirling structure designed for the more recent "Bantayan Park Center" project in the Philippines, it is literally a network. The diagram, blown up to scale 1, has finally merged with the actual building, unleashing the power of the algorithm.

*1  Mario Carpo, *The Second Digital Turn: Design Beyond Intelligence*, MIT Press, 2017.

*2  Gilles Retsin (guest editor), *Discrete: Reappraising the Digital in Architecture*, Wiley, 2019.

*3  Arata Isozaki, *Japan-ness in Architecture*, MIT Press, 2011, p. 273-274 and 286.

*4  Walter Gropius, "Architecture in Japan," in Virginia Ponciroli (ed.), *Katsura Imperial Villa*, Phaidon 2011, p. 355.

Elie During
Philospher, Paris Nanterre University.
Born in Tehran in 1972.  He studied at Sorbonne, Princeton
University and the Ecole normale superieure. He has been an associate professor at Paris Nanterre.
He famously introduced the concept of "prototype" to explore the meaning of contemporary artworks
and their emergent spatio-temporal frameworks in the age of information technologies.

# 桂離宮
## Katsura Imperial Villa

*Axonometric Drawing*

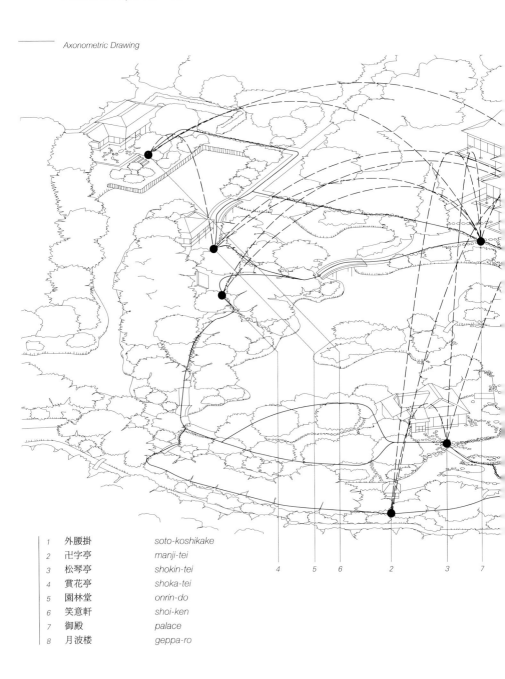

| | | |
|---|---|---|
| 1 | 外腰掛 | *soto-koshikake* |
| 2 | 卍字亭 | *manji-tei* |
| 3 | 松琴亭 | *shokin-tei* |
| 4 | 賞花亭 | *shoka-tei* |
| 5 | 園林堂 | *onrin-do* |
| 6 | 笑意軒 | *shoi-ken* |
| 7 | 御殿 | *palace* |
| 8 | 月波楼 | *geppa-ro* |

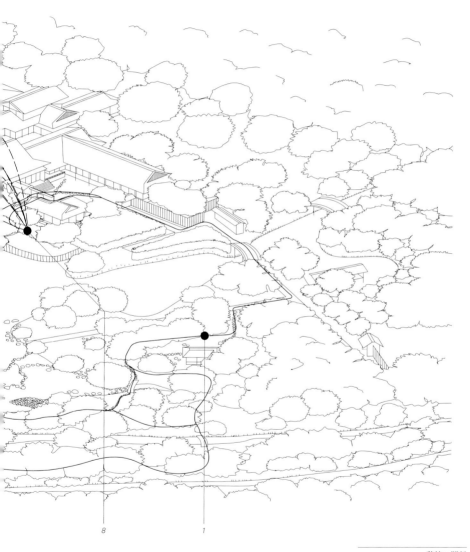

8　　　　　1

動線の関係
*connection of passage*

視線の関係
*connection of visibility*

Netwrok Diagram

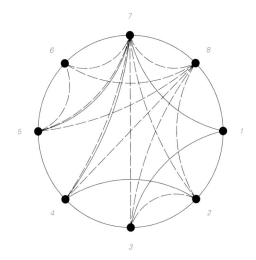

動線の関係
*connection of passage*

視線の関係
*connection of visibility*

| 1 | 外腰掛 | *soto-koshikake* |
| 2 | 卍字亭 | *manji-tei* |
| 3 | 松琴亭 | *shokin-tei* |
| 4 | 賞花亭 | *shoka-tei* |
| 5 | 園林堂 | *onrin-do* |
| 6 | 笑意軒 | *shoi-ken* |
| 7 | 御殿 | *palace* |
| 8 | 月波楼 | *geppa-ro* |

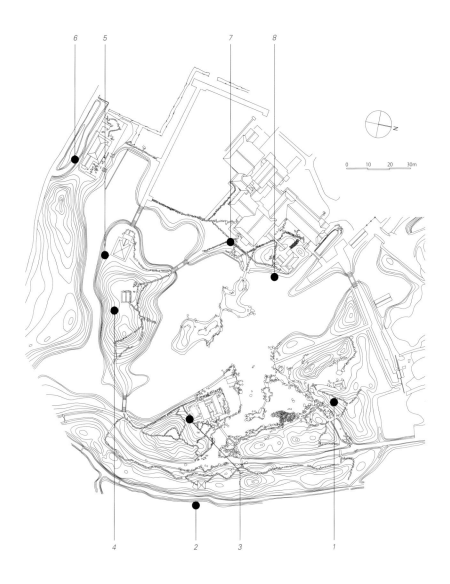

# 関係性を顕在化させるアルゴリズムによる ネットワーク型の建築
## 柄沢祐輔

## 秩序と多様性を両立させる アルゴリズム建築

コンピュータを設計に応用した建築は、現在アルゴリズム建築と呼ばれている。情報技術が浸透した私達の社会にふさわしい建築のあり方を探求する建築家は世界にも多くおり、私もそのひとりだ。そうした数多くの研究の中で、私が辿り着いたひとつの結論がある。それはアルゴリズム建築の可能性とは、「秩序」と「多様性」がともにある建築だということである。

コンピュータの登場の後と前で、一番変わったところは何だろうか。私はそれを「細かな離散系」と「粗い離散系」の対比だと考えている。コンピュータが登場する前に、人間がアナログな技術しか持ち合わせていなかった時代においては、私達は極めて粗い解像度で世界の物事を眺めていたと言える。「離散化」とは、ある連続した値を不連続な値に分割することで、たとえば世界のできごとを名指す際に、私達は 1、2、3……と自然数によって物事を指折り数えていくような行為のことを指す。離散とは「ばらばら」を意味する言葉であり、本来は分割して区別ができない無限の自然のありようを、人間が理解・把握をするために、区別する方法のことなのだ。コンピュータの登場以前は、私達はいわば「粗い離散化」の世界を生きていたと言える。この事実は、コンピュータが現れる以前には、たとえば私達が物事をデザインする際に、基本的には 1：1：1

の整数比を用いた直交座標系を利用してデザインを行っていたことに端的に表れているだろう。有史以来ほとんどの建築は、ギリシア時代のパルテノン神殿から始まって、ルネッサンス建築、近世の新古典主義の建築、近代のル・コルビュジェやミース・ファン・デル・ローエの建築に至るまで、基本的には 1：1：1 の整数比のグリッドが床面に敷かれ、その基準線を基に建築が組み立てられている。都市計画にしても同様であろう。対して、コンピュータの登場により、私達はそれ以前のアナログな方法論の時代とは全く異なる解像度で世界を眺めることが可能になった。1960 年に気象学者のエドワード・ローレンツは気象現象のモデル化に成功し、非線形のカオスのモデルが世界で最初に生み出されたが、これはコンピュータという技術なしには実現することができなかった。コンピュータの登場によって気象現象のような複雑な現象の背後にある秩序を取り出し、さまざまな自然現象のシミュレーションを行うことができるようになったのだ。これはコンピュータ以前の世界の把握とはまったく解像度の異なる、「細かな離散系」による世界の把握であると言える。

このコンピュータという「細かな離散系」の方法論によって、従来のアナログな方法論では考えもつかなかった程複雑な形態の建築やデザインが、今日次々に生み出されている。そればかりでなく、このコンピュータという「細かな離散系」の技術は、自然界が多様性に満

ちているとともに、シンプルなルール、秩序が同時に存在していることを明らかにしてきた。複雑系の科学とは、コンピュータを駆使して自然界の背後に潜むさまざまな秩序、ルールを探求する学問だが、この進展によって、自然界のさまざまな現象、たとえば気流や乱流、樹木の枝分かれ、植物の葉の並び方など一見複雑な現象の背後にシンプルなルールが存在していることが明らかになった。複雑系の科学者たちは、この多様性と秩序が絶妙なバランスでせめぎ合っている状態を「カオスの縁」と名付け、自然界のさまざまな創発現象や、生命現象の根幹に、この現象が位置づけられることを明らかにしてきた。コンピュータという「細かな離散系」の技術が可能にする建築のデザインの地平とは、この複雑系の科学が「カオスの縁」として指し示す、「秩序」と「多様性」がバランスした状態を建築のデザインとして実現することであり、この秩序と多様性がともにある状態とは、秩序が強いモダニズムまでの建築とも、また多様性だけを追い求めてきたポストモダン建築とも異なる、まったく新しい建築のデザインの地平なのである。アルゴリズム建築という分野の可能性は、まさに「秩序」と「多様性」が同時に存在する状態を建築として実現することにあるのだ。

筆者はこの立場に基づいて、2009年に《villa kanousan》という週末住宅の設計を行った。そこでは、建物の大きなキューブに無数のキューブが挿入され、それらのキューブの回転角は隣同士で

15度という値によって相互に角度が規定され、そのキューブによって天井や壁、床という空間の闊が抉り切り取られている。その結果、表面上は多様な見えがかりに溢れながらも、その背後では15度という回転角のアルゴリズムが明確に知覚される、いわば秩序と多様性がともに存在している建築空間を生み出すことができた。通常多様な角度がせめぎ合っている建築は、たとえばフランク・O・ゲーリーの建築のようにランダムな知覚しか生み出さないが、ここでは、見えがかりのさまざまな多様な角度が明確にアルゴリズムに基づいているために、表面の多様さの背後にある秩序が存在していることが明確に知覚される。この《villa kanousan》は住宅の用途として完成した建築としては、おそらくは世界でも最初のアルゴリズム建築である。

## ネットワーク型の建築をめざして

複雑系の科学は、世界そのものが複雑なネットワークであることも明らかにしつつある。1998年にアメリカの複雑ネットワークの研究者のダンカン・ワッツとスティーヴン・ストロガッツは「スモールワールド・ネットワーク」という図式を発見した (fig.1)。この図式では、一次元の格子がぐるりとループを描く中に、さまざまな点 (ノード) が近くで接続 (リンク) を遂げているが、基本的には近くの点同士が緊密に繋がっている (クラスター) ものの、部分的にほどけて一部遠くの点とも接続し

ている（ショートカット）。左側の図表はノードが近くとしか接続していない状態を指し、「秩序」の強い規則格子と呼ばれる。ここではクラスターしかない。反対に右側の図表は、ノードが遠くとしか接続していない状態を指し、「多様性・ランダム性」の強いランダム・ネットワークと呼ばれる。ここではショートカットしか存在していない。中央に位置する図表が「スモールワールド・ネットワーク」の図式であるが、この「スモールワールド・ネットワーク」の図式においては、「短い距離」（クラスター）と「長い距離」（ショートカット）がどちらに偏ることもなく同時に存在しているのである。そればかりではなく、複雑系の科学が明らかにした「カオスの縁」のように、この図式では秩序と多様性が精妙にバランスしており、そのバランスは α パラメータという数学的な変数領域によって厳密に定義されるのである。これにより、「長い距離」と「短い距離」がともに存在するというインターネットなどの情報空間で普段私達が感じるような、物理的な距離感覚を超えて、多様な距離がせめぎ合うという状態が、明確に数学的な図式として理解することが可能になったと言える。そればかりでなく、この「スモールワールド・ネットワーク」の図式は、今日では、生体の細胞ネットワーク、脳細胞、社会ネットワーク、インターネット等に至るまで私たちの身の回りに存在するありとあらゆるネットワーク構造に普遍的に見出すことが可能であることが判明している。私はこの「短い距離」と「長い距離」が同時に

存在し、「秩序」と「多様性」のバランスの取れた「スモールワールド・ネットワーク」の図式を、現実の建築空間として実現したいと考えるようになった。

　そのような試みが純粋な住宅建築として結実したのが 2013 年に完成した《s-house》である。この建物においては、空間自体が複雑に編み込まれたネットワーク型の建築空間が生み出されている。壁と床と庇は連続的に繋がり、各階の中央にはヴォイドが設けられているが、そのヴォイドの反対側の空間は、視覚的にはすぐ近くに見えるものの、実際に到達するためには物理的にぐるりと大きな迂回を経なくては辿り着くことができない。いわば視覚的に「短い距離」と物理的に「長い距離」という二つの異なる距離を同時に経験することができる空間になっている。あたかも「スモールワールド・ネットワーク」の図式のように、「短い距離」と「長い距離」が同時に経験される、特異な建築空間が生み出されることになった。《s-house》の内部では、多様な距離感が交錯し、奥行きの感覚も攪乱されるため、訪れる人は実際の空間の大きさよりも大きな空間を知覚することができるようになっている。

　このようなネットワーク型の空間を、今後も追求していきたいと考えている。本書において、ネットワーク図が幾つかのプロジェクトの図面の横に配置されているが、このネットワーク図では、点は各室を表し、実線は物理的なネットワークとしての動線の関係を意味し、破線が視覚的なネットワークとしての空間の繋

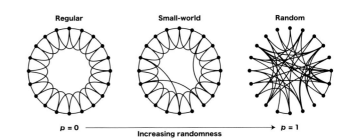

fig.1

1998 年にダンカン・ワッツとスティーヴン・ストロガッツによって
発見された〈スモールワールド・ネットワーク〉図式

がりを意味している。物理的な距離と視覚的な距離という二つの異なる距離が錯綜し、ネットワークとしての多様な関係が生み出されているさまを表現している。各プロジェクトの解説の脇には、形態形成の論理を三次元のアイコンとして図示している。アルゴリズムによるネットワーク型の建築というコンセプトによって、いかに複雑で豊かな関係が建築空間の内部に生み出されているかを本書に収められたネットワーク図とアイコン、CG や写真のヴィジュアルとともに視覚的に体験していただければと願っている。

このアルゴリズムによるネットワーク型の建築とは、果たしてどのような意味を持っているのか。それは一言で言うならば、「関係性を顕在化させる」建築であると言えるだろう。三次元的に編み込まれ、複雑に入り組んだ建築空間の中に

身を置いた人は、そこで普段見慣れた事物や人を、意外な視点や角度から眺めることによって、さまざまな発見をすることになるだろう。それは自然の中で人が川の流れや風のそよぎ、木々のざわめき、見たことのない草花、などさまざまな発見をしていくことに似ている。アルゴリズムによるネットワーク型の建築の経験というのは、こうした経験に似ている。私達の身の回りには実に沢山の関係性が隠れている。発見とは、その隠れた関係性が私たちの前に顕在化することにほかならない。アルゴリズムによるネットワーク型の空間の中をさまようとき、人は隠れた関係性が次から次へと顕在化してゆくことに、気が付くだろう。そんな発見に満ちたアルゴリズムによるネットワーク型の建築を、私はさまざまな形でそっと世の中に埋め込んでゆきたいと考えている。

# Network-type architecture by algorithms reveals relationships
# Yuusuke Karasawa

## Algorithmic architecture that balances order and diversity

The architecture that uses computers to design is now called algorithmic architecture. There are many architects in the world who are searching for an ideal form and type of architecture that suits our increasingly IT-savvy societies. I am one of them. Through various studies and research on the theme, I have come to a conclusion: algorithmic architecture is the architecture in which "order" and "diversity" can coexist.

What is the most significant change the advent of computers has brought? I would say it is the availability of "high-resolution discrete systems" as opposed to "coarse discrete systems". Before computers when we had only analog technologies, we saw the world at fairly coarse resolutions. "Discretization" is the act of dividing a continuous value into discontinuous values. For example, when referring to events or phenomena in the world, we count them using natural numbers (ex. 1, 2, 3…) as if they were something countable on our fingers. "Discrete" means "disjointed", and it is a way of comprehending the infinite nature that can not be divided per se. Before computers, we lived in the world of "coarse discretization". Back then, when designing for instance, we basically used a Cartesian coordinate system with the integer ratio of 1:1:1. Over the course of recorded history, from the Parthenon of Ancient Greece to Renaissance architecture, neoclassicism in the early modern period and architectures of

Le Corbusier and Mies van der Rohe in the late modern period, most of the architectures were created basically by laying a grid with the integer ratio of 1:1:1 on the floor and constructing the building based on the grid lines. The same goes for city plannings. The advent of computers has enabled us to see the world at a completely different resolution from that of times of analog methodologies. In 1960, meteorologist Edward Lorenz succeeded in modeling a meteorological phenomenon and developed a non-linear model of chaos for the first time in history, which would not have been possible without computer technology. By using computers, it became possible to find order in complicated phenomena such as meteorological phenomena and to simulate various natural phenomena. In other words, we can now comprehend the world through "high-resolution discrete systems", which is a completely different way of seeing the world from that of times before computers.

Today by using this methodology of "high-resolution discrete systems", that is computers, highly complex architectures and designs that were not even imaginable with conventional analog methodologies are being created. Moreover, the technology of "high-resolution discrete systems", again that is computers, has revealed that while the natural world has a great diversity, simple rules and orders exist at the same time. Complex systems science is a discipline that uses computers to study various orders and rules inherent in nature. Thanks to the progress in such studies, it has become evident that simple rules exist in various seemingly complex natural phenomena such as airstreams, turbulence, branching of trees and arrangements of leaves. Scientists of complex systems named this state in which diversity and order are facing each other in an exquisite balance the "edge of chaos" and have revealed that it constitutes the basis of various emergent phenomena and life phenomena in the natural world. The technology of "high-resolution discrete systems", i.e. computers, enables us to create this "edge of chaos", the state in which "order" and "diversity" coexist in a fine balance, as an architectural design, and such a state is a completely new horizon in the field of architectural design, different from both architectures up to modernism where order is stronger and postmodern architectures where only diversity was pursued. The greatest potentiality of algorithmic architecture resides in its ability to create a state in which both "order" and "diversity" exist as an architecture. From this perspective, I designed a weekend house "villa kanousan" in 2009. In this building, a great number of cubes are inserted into a large cube that constitutes the exterior of the building. The rotation angle of each cube is 15 degrees against the adjacent cube, and those cubes create openings in the ceilings, walls and floors. As a result, the algorithm of the rotation angle of 15 degree is clearly perceived while the interior has diverse appearances, thus creating an architectural space where order and diversity coexist.

Generally, structures with a variety of angles such as those of Frank O. Gehry's produce only random perceptions. Here, however, since the diverse angles that are visible are all based on the algorithm, one can perceive a certain order in the full diverseness of the appearance. "villa kanousan" is probably the first algorithmic architecture in the world that was built for residential use.

## Pursuing
## the network-type architecture

Complex systems science is also revealing that the world itself is a complex network. In 1998, American researchers of complex networks, Duncan Watts and Steven Strogatz developed the scheme of "Small World Network" (fig.1). In this scheme, a one-dimensional lattice draws a circle, and points (nodes) are placed on its circumference. Each of those nodes is basically connected (link) to its neighbors (cluster), but some of them are partially untied from their neighbors and connected to those far from them as well (shortcut). The diagram on the left shows the state in which nodes are connected only to their neighbors. In this state, "order" dominates. It is called regular lattice and there are only clusters in it. The diagram on the right shows the state in which nodes are only connected to those far from them. In this state, "diversity / randomness" dominates. It is called random network and there are only shortcuts in it. The one in the middle is the diagram of "Small World Network" in which both "short distance" (cluster) and "long distance" (shortcut) exist in a fine balance. Moreover, order and diversity are exquisitely balanced in this chart as in the "edge of chaos" revealed by complex systems science, and this balance is strictly defined by a mathematical variable area called "alpha" parameter. Thus it is now possible to seize as a mathematical scheme the state where various relationships of distance exist together as if we experience in the information space like the Internet which both "long distance" and "short distance" exist simultaneously. Furthermore, it has been proved that this "Small World Network" scheme can be universally found in all kinds of network structures around us such as biological cellular networks, brain cells, social networks and the Internet. This leads me to an idea of creating the "Small World Network" in which both "short distance" and "long distance" exist simultaneously and "order" and "diversity" are balanced as a real architectural space.

Resulted from this attempt is "s-house": a residential building which was completed in 2013. In this building, a network-type architectural space where the space itself is intricately woven is created. The walls, floors and eaves are connected in continuity and there is a void at the center of each floor. The space on the opposite side of the void is visually close but you can only reach it by taking a long detour. In other words, it is a space where you can experience a visually "short distance" and a physically "long distance" at the same time. It is a unique architectural space where "short

distance" and "long distance" can be experienced at the same time as in the "Small World Network" scheme. Inside "s-house", various senses of distance intersect and the sense of depth is disturbed, therefore visitors can feel as if the space were larger than the actual size.

It is my challenge to continue pursuing the network-type space. In this book, network diagrams are shown next to the drawings of some of the projects. In these diagrams, each dot represents a room, the solid lines represent the relationships of flow lines as a physical network, and the dashed lines describe the connection of spaces as a visual network. They show how these two kinds of distance, physical and visual, entwine, creating various relationships as a network. Next to the text of each project, the logic of morphogenesis is depicted in a three dimensional icon. I hope that this book, with its network schemes, icons, CG and photographs, will help the readers visually experience the rich and complex relationships created in the architectural space by the concept of network-type architecture by algorithms.

What does network-type architecture by algorithms mean? In a word, it would be the "architecture that reveals relationships". In an intricate three-dimensionally-woven architectural space, one will make various new discoveries by looking at familiar things and people from different perspectives and unexpected angles. It is similar to what we experience in nature when we

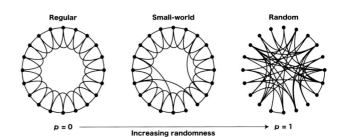

fig.1

Diagram of Small World Network which was found
by Duncan Watts and Steven Strogatz in1998

discover a flow of a river, feel a breeze, hear a rustle of trees, or find flowers that we have never seen before. Network-type architecture by algorithms provides us with that kind of experience. There are so many relationships hidden around us. A discovery takes place when those hidden relationships manifest themselves before us. When wandering through a network-type architectural space created by algorithms, you will see hidden relationships reveal themselves one after another. I would like to embed in the world various network-type architectures by algorithms full of such discoveries.

# ウェブデザイナーの
# オフィス・インテリア
# Interior Design for Web Designer

*2006 Tokyo*

## 無限に伸長する
## 素数のグリッド
*A grid of prime numbers extending infinitely*

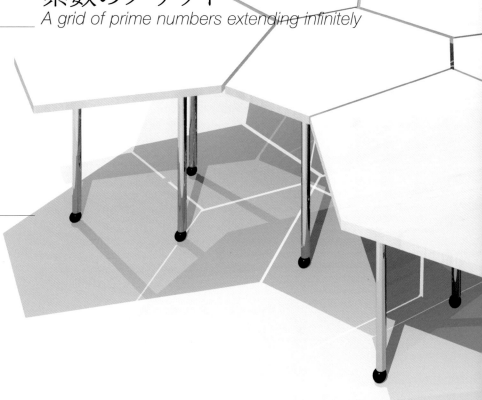

*Three Dimensional Icon*

空間を無限に反復する
イレギュラーなエレメント

周期的反復
*repetition*

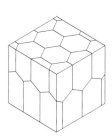

Irregular elements which infinitely
repeat itself in space

ウェブデザイナー集団のオフィスのミーティング・テーブルである。一辺が素数によってできた「素数のジオメトリー」をデザインした。ばらしてひとつのテーブルとして用いることもでき、また集めて一体のテーブルとして用いることもできる。デザインした幾何学には周期性があるため、空間を無限に反復しながら埋め尽くすことができる。

This is a meeting table in an office space for a group of web designers. Designed as a "geometry of prime numbers" in which length of each side of the table is made up of a prime number, it can be used as a single table by disassembling its composing pieces, or as one large table by assembling them together. Since designed geometry has its periodic cycle, space may be filled with infinitely repeating geometry.

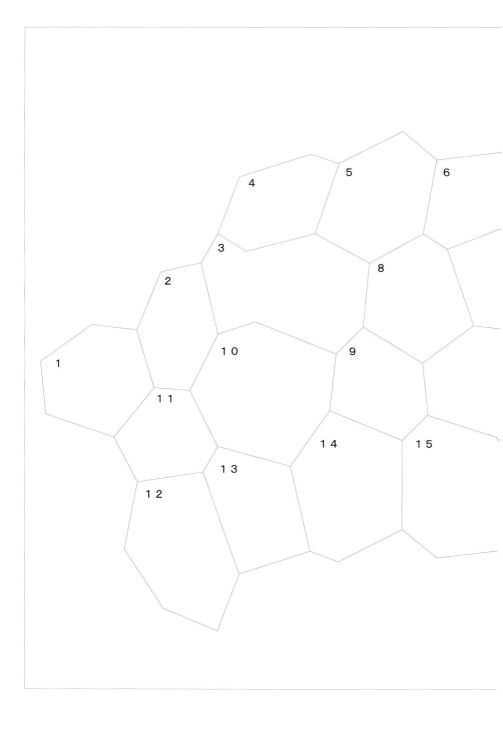

| | | | | | | | | | |
|---|---|---|---|---|---|---|---|---|---|
| 2 | 3 | 5 | 7 | 11 | 13 | 17 | 19 | 23 | 29 |
| 31 | 37 | 41 | 43 | 47 | 53 | 59 | 61 | 67 | 71 |
| 73 | 79 | 83 | 89 | 97 | 101 | 103 | 107 | 109 | 113 |
| 127 | 131 | 137 | 139 | 149 | 151 | 157 | 163 | 167 | 173 |
| 179 | 181 | 191 | 193 | 197 | 199 | 211 | 223 | 227 | 229 |
| 233 | 239 | 241 | 251 | 257 | 263 | 269 | 271 | 277 | 281 |
| 283 | 293 | 307 | 311 | 313 | 317 | 331 | 337 | 347 | 349 |
| 353 | 359 | 367 | 373 | 379 | 383 | 389 | 397 | 401 | 409 |
| 419 | 421 | 431 | 433 | 439 | 443 | 449 | 457 | 461 | 463 |
| 467 | 479 | 487 | 491 | 499 | 503 | 509 | 521 | 523 | 541 |
| 547 | 557 | 563 | 569 | 571 | 577 | 587 | 593 | 599 | 601 |
| 607 | 613 | 617 | 619 | 631 | 641 | 643 | 647 | 653 | 659 |
| 661 | 673 | 677 | 683 | 691 | 701 | 709 | 719 | 727 | 733 |
| 739 | 743 | 751 | 757 | 761 | 769 | 773 | 787 | 797 | 809 |
| 811 | 821 | 823 | 827 | 829 | 839 | 853 | 857 | 859 | 863 |
| 877 | 881 | 883 | 887 | 907 | 911 | 919 | 929 | 937 | 941 |
| 947 | 953 | 967 | 971 | 977 | 983 | 991 | 997 | 1009 | 1013 |

7

1/20

1/50

| Project : | primary number scale assembled meeting desks | 2006.Oct.16 | No. |
|---|---|---|---|
| Title : | drawing of the assemblies | 1:50   1:20 | 01 |
| **primary desk** | | table on periodical geometory consists of primary numbers | |

# 秋葉原駅前
# 再開発プロジェクト
Redevelopment Plan in Front of

*2006 Tokyo*

フーリエ変換による
人工の風景
*Artificial landscape by Fourier transform*

PLEATS
PLEASE

*Three Dimensional Icon*

周期的に凹凸を
繰り返す人工地盤

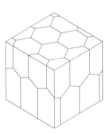

周期的反復
*repetition*

Artificial ground with repeating
concavo-convex

秋葉原駅前のJRの高架下 4500 ㎡の再開発の計画である。ここではフーリエ変換によって音楽のデータをサインウェーブに変換して波型の幾何学を取り出し、その幾何学を用いて周期的に凹凸を繰り返す立体的なパターンをもつ人工地盤をつくり、盛り上がった部分には歩行者用通路、くぼんで囲われた部分には様々な小型の店舗を収めた。秋葉原の高密度な商店街を未来的な風景として再構成することを試みた。

This is a 4,500 square-meter redevelopment project under the elevated JR Akihabara Station railway line. By converting musical data to sine waves with Fourier transformation, we have extracted the waveform geometry with which we created an artificial ground with a three-dimensional repeating concavo-convex pattern. The raised area constructs a ceiling of a pedestrian walkway, and the concaved enclosed area constructs a floor for a variety of small stores. This is an attempt to reconstruct the high-density shopping district of Akihabara with a futuristic landscape.

# 尾山台の家

## House in Oyamadai

*2006 Tokyo*

### モーフィングによる
### トップライトの空間

*A space with a morphing skylight*

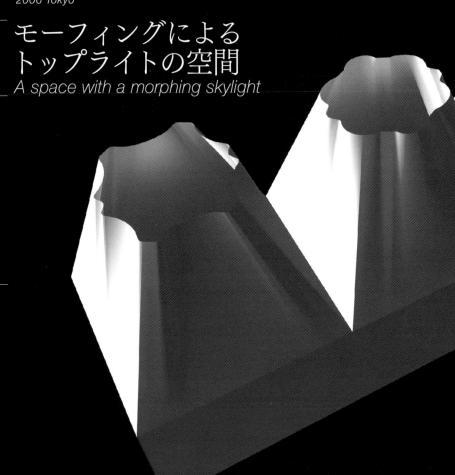

*Three Dimensional Icon*

直交する幾何学と
歪曲する幾何学のモーフィング

モーフィング
*morphing*

Morphing of orthogonal and
distortional geometries

世田谷の狭小住宅地に計画された小住宅である。三方を住宅に取り囲まれた
細分化された敷地であるため、思い切って大型のトップライトから空に向けての
眺望を採っている。建築空間は天井に埋め込まれた非ユークリッド幾何学のジ
オメトリーと、床面のユークリッド幾何学のジオメトリーをモーフィングすることによ
って生み出されている。

This is a micro housing in a small residential district in Setagaya, Tokyo. Since the
subdivided plot is surrounded closely by houses on three sides, we developed
a large skylight which allows a wide view to the sky. The architectural space is
created by morphing the non-Euclidean geometry engraved in the ceiling and the
Euclidean geometry on the floor.

# villa kanousan

## villa kanousan

*2009 Chiba*

刻々と変化する
キューブによるヴォイド
*Void from gradually transforming cubes*

*Three Dimensional Icon*

アルゴリズムで定義された
キューブによって
ヴォリュームを刳りぬく

ブーリアン
*boolean*

Subtracting architectural
volume with algorithmically
defined cubes

房総半島中部、君津市鹿野山の山深い別荘地にある週末住宅である。かつて日本画家の東山魁夷がその光景を眺めて風景画に目覚めたといわれる雄大な渓谷を見下ろす傾斜地にこの建物は佇んでいる。建物の外形は単純なキューブであるが、内部は伝統的な田の字平面が二層に重ねられ、その空間を仕切る壁面と床面と天井の交点にキューブが貫入し、空間の閾を抉り切り取っている。それぞれのキューブ同士の角度はアルゴリズムによって規定されており、隣接するキューブの角度が15度という一定の値でずれている点が最大の方法論的特徴となっている。このようにアルゴリズムで定義されたキューブの回転角によって各空間が切り取られ、その切断面によってそれぞれの室に個別の空間的特徴が生み出されている。空間はそれぞれに多様な表情を持ちつつも、キューブの角度の設定がランダムな操作ではないために一定の秩序感が建物全体に与えられ、秩序とともにある多様性という二律背反的な経験を身体感覚として味わうことが可能な空間となっている。日中は天井に設えられたトップライトからの光が室内に差し込み、予想しない方向から光線が内部空間で交錯し、多様な空間がさらに豊かな表情を醸し出す。時間によっては、光が壁面によって分散し、さまざまな色に分かれて室内を照らし出す。建物全体がさながら天然のプリズムと化す。キューブの回転角の初期値が敷地の傾斜角に合わせて設定されていることで、周囲の雄大な自然の風景を集約して空間内部に取り込み、外部との一体感を内部に訪れる者に与える。周囲の環境と呼応した、秩序とともに多様性を感じることができる、全く新しい空間がアルゴリズムの方法論によって生み出されることになった。

This is a weekend getaway house situated in a deep mountainous villa area of Kimitsu-city, located in the center of Boso Peninsula. It is tucked away in a sloping lot overlooking a valley where late Japanese painter Kaii Higashiyama (1908-99) is said to have been awakened to landscape painting by the majestic view of the valley.

While the architectural form is a simple cube, the interior is composed of two floors of traditional *tanoji*-shaped (crossed square) plan, with cubes penetrating the intersection of the wall, floor and ceiling partitioning the spatial threshold.

The biggest methodological feature of this house is the angles between cubes defined by a specific algorithm, where each cube is rotated by 15 degrees to its adjacent one. The partition of each space is subtracted by the cubes which rotation angle is defined by algorithm and it creates space which is filled with diverse characteristic for each room. Although each space has a different expression, there is a certain sense of order throughout the entire house as the angles of the cubes are not set at random but defined by algorithm, allowing the antithetical experience of diversity with order as a physical sensation. During daytime, natural light from the skylight enters the interior, emphasizing a richer expression of diverse spaces as rays of light intersect in the interior space from unexpected directions. Depending on the time of day, the light is dispersed by the walls and illuminates the interior in various colors. Thus, the entire house becomes like a natural prism. By setting the default rotation angle of the cube according to the sloping gradient of the site, the magnificent natural scenery is introduced into the interior of the space, which gives visitors a sense of unity with the outside. The algorithm methodology created a completely new space that responds to the surrounding environment and allows for a sense of order and diversity.

*Netwrok Diagram*

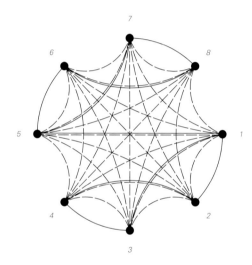

動線の関係
*connection of passage*

視線の関係
*connection of visibility*

| | | |
|---|---|---|
| 1 | 玄関ホール | *entrance hall* |
| 2 | キッチン | *kitchen* |
| 3 | 書斎 | *study room* |
| 4 | リビングルーム | *living room* |
| 5 | 階段室 | *staircase* |
| 6 | ゲストルーム | *guest room* |
| 7 | 浴室・トイレ | *bath and toilet* |
| 8 | ベッドルーム | *bedroom* |

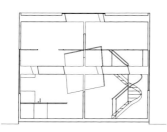

*A-A' section*

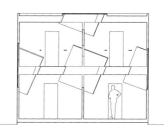

*B-B' section*

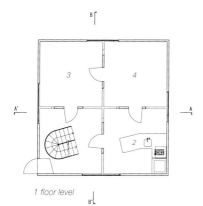

*1 floor level*

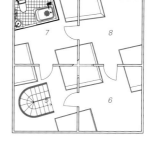

*2 floor level*

# 中心が移動し続ける都市
## City of Permanently Shifting Center

*2009 Tokyo*

## 格差を是正する都市のアルゴリズム
*Urban algorithms to redress disparity*

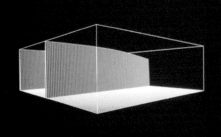

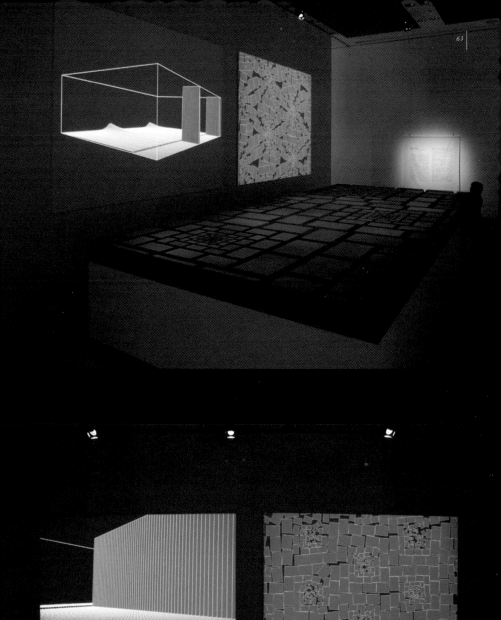

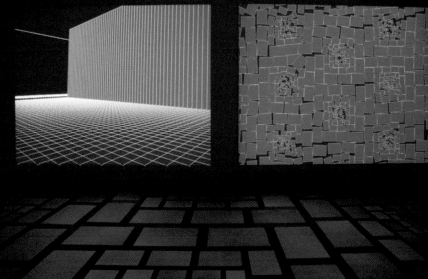

*Three Dimensional Icon*

フィボナッチ級数による
多極中心のヴォリュームが
反復する都市計画

周期的反復
*repetition*

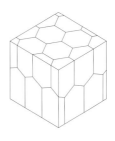

フィボナッチ
*fibonacci*

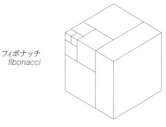

Urban planning with repeating
multipole-centric volumes by
Fibonacci series

NTTインターコミュニケーション・センター (ICC) での都市計画のインスタレーション。ノーベル経済学賞を受賞したポール・クルーグマンは、著書『自己組織化の経済学』(1996) において、都市が、時間の経過と共に繁栄する一部の中心地とその周辺で衰退する郊外へと次第に自己組織化するプロセスの説明を行っている。ここでは、繁栄する中心と衰退する郊外がどのように分岐するかをシミュレーションによって計測し、その格差が拭いがたく固定化した瞬間に、中心地が衰退している郊外へと移動していく都市計画のモデルをソフトウェアとして実装した。現実の都市空間の背後で作動する、経済の自己組織化のメカニズムに関与する新しい都市計画のあり方を提示している。

This is an installation of urban planning at the NTT Intercommunication Center (ICC). The Nobel Prize winner in economics Paul Krugman explains in his book "The Self-Organizing Economy (1996)" the process in which some metropolis thrives with the passage of time, whereas its surrounding regions gradually self-organize to declining suburbs. In this installation, we simulated how a thriving metropolis and a declining suburb diverge. This installation implemented a software of an urban planning model in which the center of metropolis moves to the declining suburbs at the moment the disparity becomes certain. It suggests a new way of urban planning that get engaged with the mechanism of economic self-organization that operates behind the real urban space.

# 瀋陽市
# 方城地区計画
## Shenyang Fangcheng Project

*2009 Shenyang,China*

## フィボナッチ級数による
## 大規模地下動線
*Large scale underground passage derived from Fibonacci*

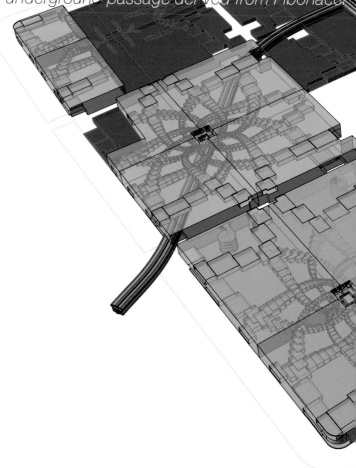

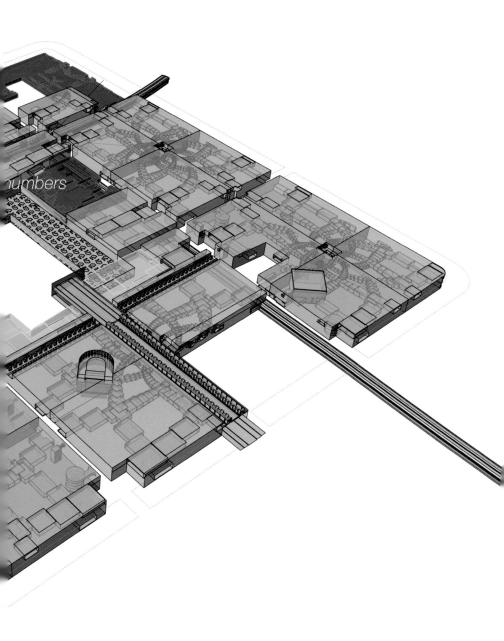

*numbers*

*Three Dimensional Icon*

編みこみ
*weave*

フィボナッチ級数によって
定義され、編み込まれた
虚のヴォリューム

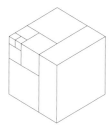

フィボナッチ
*fibonacci*

Woven Imaginary volumes
defined by Fibonacci numbers

ブーリアン
*boolean*

中国瀋陽市の中心部に位置する世界遺産の瀋陽故宮を中心とした都市開発の計画である。開発面積は 1.2 km 四方の旧市街全体、約 120 万㎡に及ぶ。故宮が低層であるため、景観保全のために旧市街全体に高さ制限が設けられている。本計画においてはその制限をより一層強調し、北京や上海など中国の各都市で展開する超高層建築を主体とした垂直型の都市開発モデルとはちがう、よりサスティナブルでエネルギー効率のよい地下空間を主に利用する大規模都市開発を立案した。計画を統括する大きな軸として、大規模な空間が単調にならないようにするため、多様な差異を孕んだフィボナッチ級数のジオメトリーが立体的に錯綜しながら絡み合うというアルゴリズムによって地下空間をデザインした。フィボナッチ数列で角度が定義された幾何学が上がり下がりを繰り返しながら編み込まれ、その幾何学を元に直方体のヴォイドが連続的に拡大縮小を繰り広げ、縦横無尽に接続される。これが地中を回遊するための大規模ネットワーク動線として活用され、その周囲に商店街、オフィス、居住施設、文化施設などが配置される。屋上にはさざ波のようなアルゴリズムによって自然の地形のような起伏に富む緑化した庭園がデザインされ、要所に回遊動線が張り巡らされる。

This is an urban development project centered on the Shenyang Palace, a World Heritage Site located in the center of Shenyang city, China. This 1.2-kilometer square old town development area covers approximately 1.2 million square-meters. Since the imperial palace is a low-rise building, height restrictions have been imposed on the entire old city to preserve its historical landscape. In this plan, by further emphasizing the height limitation, a large-scale urban development was planned to utilize mainly the underground space that is more sustainable and energy efficient unlike the vertical urban development models of Beijing, Shanghai and other Chinese cities that focus mainly on developing skyscrapers. A major axis governing the plan is the design of the underground space using an algorithm in which the geometries derived from Fibonacci series with variances area intertwined in a three-dimensional complex. Based on the repeatedly woven geometries with angles defined by the Fibonacci series, continuously scaling rectangular voids are connected in all directions. These voids are utilized as a large-scale network flow line that circulates underground, and shops, offices, residential and cultural facilities are attached to the voids. On the rooftop, a green undulating garden derived from a ripple-like algorithm is designed to resemble a natural terrain.

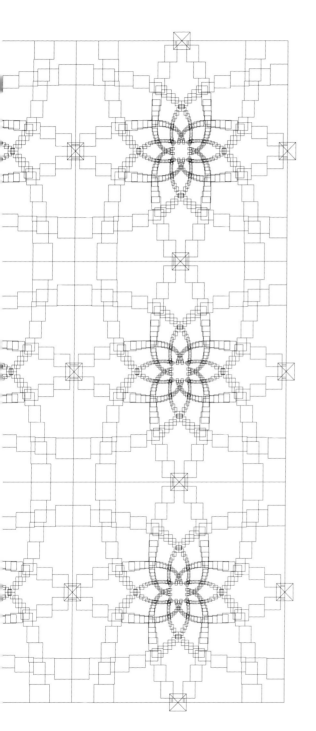

# s-house

## s-house

2013  Saitama

三次元的に
複雑に編み込まれた空間
Complicatedly woven three-dimensional space

編みこみ
*weave*

*Three Dimensional Icon*

編み込まれ、
枝分れと合流を繰り広げる
レイヤー状の空間

枝分かれ
*branch*

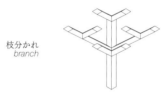

周期的反復
*repetition*

A layered space which is
interwoven and repeats
diversion and convergence

レイヤー
*layering*

埼玉県大宮駅にほど近い住宅地に建てられた狭小住宅である。100㎡程の敷地に、約50㎡の床が2層に渡って空中に掛け渡されているが、各層は平面で4分割され、その4分割された床のうち2面が半階分持ち上げられ、同じ高さで張り巡らされた庇が、持ち上げられた床面と連続しながら絡み合い、複雑に編み込まれたネットワーク型の空間を生み出している。床面は枝分かれして他の床と合流を繰り返し、外部の庇と互い違いに取り合いながら、独自の絡み合った立面を構成している。立面のみならず内部空間においてもこの錯綜する構成の論理は貫徹しており、床自体が対角線上に絡み合い交錯し、その中心部には反対側の空間が望めるヴォイドが生み出されている。このヴォイドを通して対角線上に見える空間は視覚的には連続しているが、その空間に辿りつくためには立体的に錯綜する層を移動し、他の床面に移動したあとにぐるりと動線を迂回しなくてはならない。いわば視覚的には近接しているものの、動線としては大きな移動距離が設定されているという、通常の建築における距離感と奥行の知覚が攪乱されるこの環境は、あたかもインターネット等の情報空間のようなさまざまな距離の関係性が多様に錯綜する建築空間を生み出している。このように多様な距離の関係が錯綜するネットワーク型の空間のあり方を、この建築物では複数の層がネットワーキングされながら積層されてゆく空間に置き換え、「複雑な階層状のネットワーク」として実現している。このような空間のあり方が、今日の情報化によって生み出された多様性と秩序が共に求められる社会における、さまざまなアクティビティを受け止める新たな建築の形式となるのではないかと期待している。

This is a small house built in a residential area near Omiya Station in Saitama prefecture, Japan. On a site of around 100 square-meters, two layers of floors of approximately 50 square-meters in size are bridged in the air. However, each floor is divided into four sections, two of which are raised half a floor height. A series of eaves stretching at the same height are intertwined with the raised floors to create a complicatedly woven network of spaces.

The floor surfaces repeatedly diverge and converge with other floors, interacting with the exterior eaves to form a unique intertwined elevation. This complex compositional logic is carried through not only on the building elevation but also in the interior spaces, where the floor itself intertwines and intersects diagonally, creating a void at the center of which allows to see the opposite side of the space.

In order to reach the space seen opposite diagonally through this void, one must make a long detour moving through the complex three-dimensional layer of space to another floor level although opposite side of the void can be seen so closely.

In this space, what appears close visually is physically far away, so short distance and long distance exist simultaneously, thus it confuses our ordinary perception of distance and depth in architecture. It creates architectural space with various complex relationships of distance, just like the Internet and other information space. Then a new form of architecture "complex hierarchical network" is developed by turning such space that is networked with intricate relationships between various distances into a space in which multiple layers are networked and stacked in the building. We expect such kind of space to be a new form of architecture that can accommodate a variety of activities in a society that demands diversity and order of today's information society.

*Axonometric Drawing*

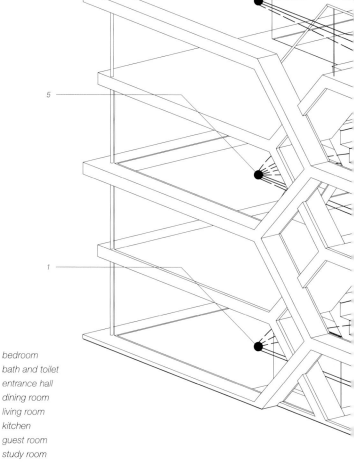

| 1 | ベッドルーム | *bedroom* |
|----|------------------|------------------|
| 2 | 浴室・トイレ | *bath and toilet* |
| 3 | 玄関ホール | *entrance hall* |
| 4 | ダイニングルーム | *dining room* |
| 5 | リビングルーム | *living room* |
| 6 | キッチン | *kitchen* |
| 7 | ゲストルーム | *guest room* |
| 8 | 書斎 | *study room* |
| 9 | 屋外テラス | *roof terrace* |
| 10 | 屋外テラス | *roof terrace* |
| 11 | 屋外テラス | *roof terrace* |
| 12 | 屋外テラス | *roof terrace* |

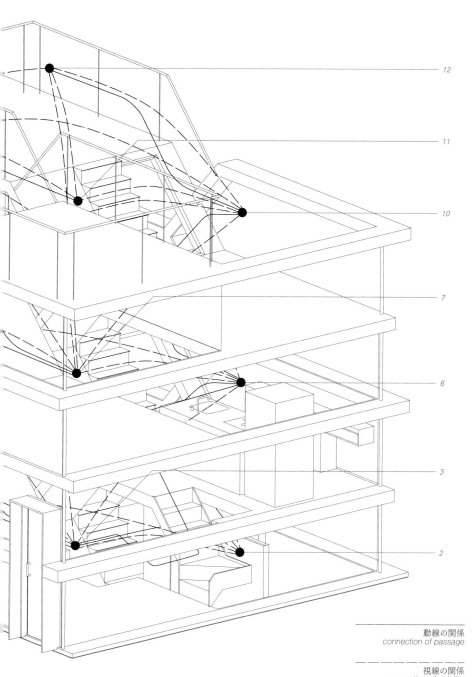

12

11

10

7

6

3

2

動線の関係
*connection of passage*

視線の関係
*connection of visibility*

Netwrok Diagram

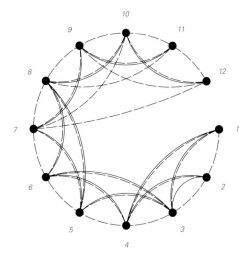

動線の関係
connection of passage

視線の関係
connection of visibility

| 1 | ベッドルーム | bedroom |
| 2 | 浴室・トイレ | bath and toilet |
| 3 | 玄関ホール | entrance hall |
| 4 | ダイニングルーム | dining room |
| 5 | リビングルーム | living room |
| 6 | キッチン | kitchen |
| 7 | ゲストルーム | guest room |
| 8 | 書斎 | study room |
| 9 | 屋外テラス | roof terrace |
| 10 | 屋外テラス | roof terrace |
| 11 | 屋外テラス | roof terrace |
| 12 | 屋外テラス | roof terrace |

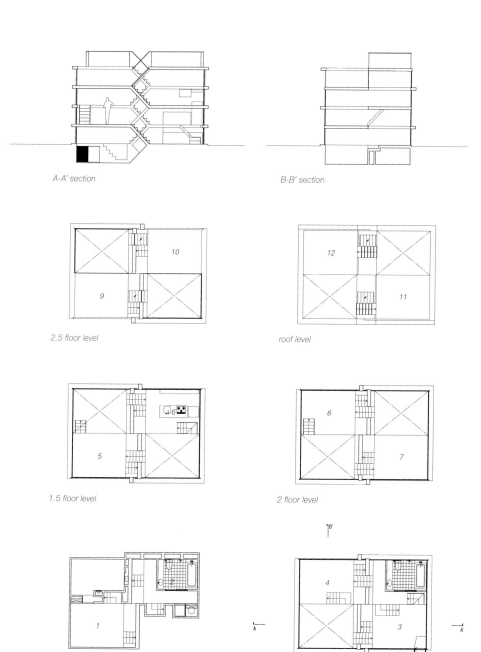

A-A' section

B-B' section

2.5 floor level

roof level

1.5 floor level

2 floor level

-0.5 floor level

1 floor level

# バンタヤン
# パークセンター
## Bantayan Park Center

2014- Bago,Philippines

# 小さな渦の連鎖により生まれる
# 大きな渦
*A large vortex composed of a chain of small vortexes*

*Three Dimensional Icon*

ずらして編み込まれた
自由曲面のエレメントが
円環をなす

編みこみ
*weave*

モーフィング
*morphing*

A circle of free-from element by
shifting and weaving

フィリピンのネグロス島の中西部にあるバゴ市の中心に位置するバンタヤン公園で現在建設が進められている公共建築のプロジェクトである。この建物ではこの公園で行政が市民のために提供している多様なプログラムが展開される。立体的な渦のようにして生み出された多目的な空間の屋根と床面の一部がほどけて、全体としても大きな渦のようにネットワーク状にリンクし合い、中央には屋外の広場が生まれる。いわば多様なアクティビティを受け止める器としてのネットワーク型の建築空間が目指されている。構造はマホガニーを用いた木造であり、湾曲した壁面は 2 インチの厚さのマホガニーを積層して作られている。屋根の材は同じくマホガニーであるが、壁の構造と屋根の構造が互いに支え合うことによって構造として成立するというネットワーク型の構造が生み出されている。2 インチのマホガニー材はすべての層において異なる曲率を持つ平面形状で切断され、各層において少しずつずらされながら積層される。そのマホガニーの各層がボルトによって緊結されることにより、極薄の木の自由曲面による構造体が実現している。この建築は、観光案内所やゲストルームとしての機能も担うことが予定されている。いわばバゴ市という共同体のためのコミュニティセンターとバゴ市の外から訪れる来訪者のための空間が重ね合わされることによって、バゴ市という共同体の内と外のインターフェイスとなる建築が目指されている。このような街の内と外のインターフェイスとしての建築が地域のアイデンティティを確たるものとし、地域の発展を促すことが期待される。

This is a public building project currently under construction in Bantayan Park, located in the heart of Bago city in the mid-western part of Negros Island, Philippines. The building unfurls a variety of programs that the government is providing for its citizens in the park. Since a roof and floor of this multi-purpose space created like a three-dimensional whirlpool is partially uncoiled, the whole space is linked together like a big whirlpool network, thus creating an open-air plaza in the center. In other words, it is intended to create a networked architectural space that serves as a vessel for a variety of activities. The structure is made of mahogany and curved wall is composed of stacking layers of two-inch thickness mahogany lumbers. While the roof structure is also made of mahogany lumber, the roof structures and wall structures depend on each other to configure structure as a whole composing network-type structure. The two-inch mahogany lumber is cut in planes of different curvature in all layers and stacked with a slight shift between each layer. Each layer of mahogany is bolted together to create a structure of ultra-thin, free-form lumber. The building will also function as a tourist information center and guest room. By superimposing a community center for Bago city and a space for visitors from outside the city, the building is intended to be an interface between the inside and outside of the community of Bago. Such architecture is expected to strengthen the identity of the local community and promote its further development.

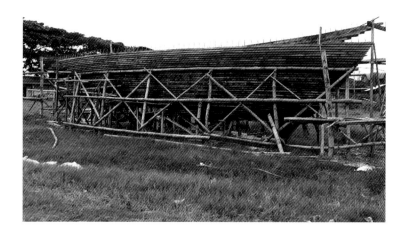

Netwrok Diagram

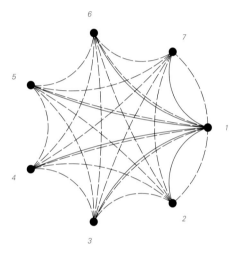

6

7

5

1

4

2

3

動線の関係
connection of passage

視線の関係
connection of visibility

| 1 | 屋外庭園 | outside garden |
| 2 | 中庭 | courtyard |
| 3 | リビングルーム | living room |
| 4 | スタディルーム | study room |
| 5 | ベッドルーム | bedroom |
| 6 | キッチン | kitchen |
| 7 | ダイニングルーム | dining room |

*north elevation*

*south elevation*

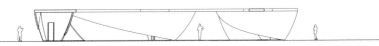

*A-A' section*

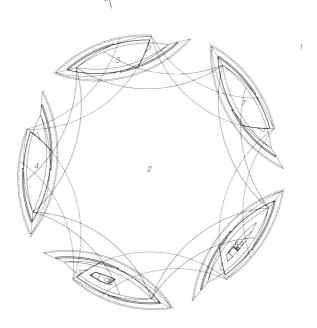

*1 floor level*

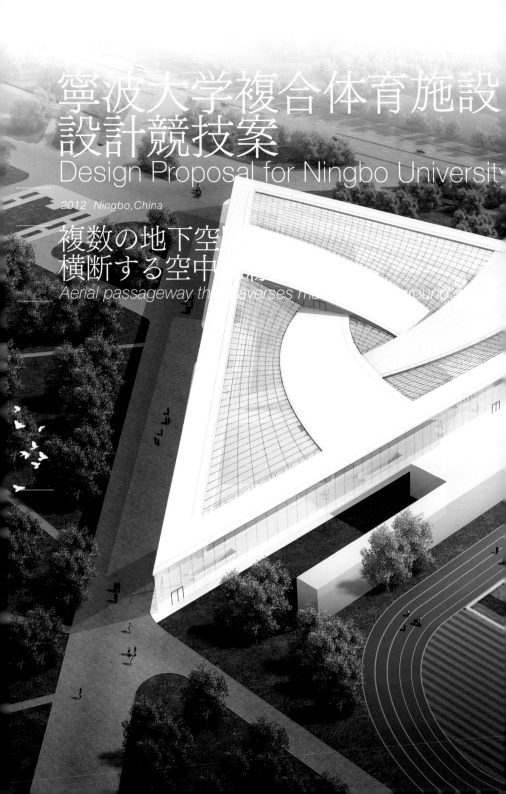

# 寧波大学複合体育施設設計競技案

Design Proposal for Ningbo Universit

2012  Ningbo,China

複数の地下空
横断する空中

*Aerial passageway th*

Gymnasium Complex

*Three Dimensional Icon*

地下のグリッド空間の上に
重ねられた編み込まれた
空中動線

編みこみ
*weave*

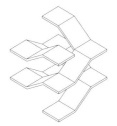

レイヤー
*layering*

Interwoven aerial passageway
overlaid above the underground
grid space

中国の浙江省の寧波市の東に位置する寧波大学の複合体育施設の設計競技案である。約18000㎡の敷地に、8000㎡もの面積をもつ主体育館とバスケットボール、バレーボール、空手、ヨガ、テコンドー、エアロビクス、体操など合計10種目のスポーツのための個別の競技場が収められる。主体育館とそれぞれ壁面で隔てられた競技場を、グリッドによって割り付けされた地下空間に収め、1階のエントランスを入ると眼下に体育館と個別の競技場を見下ろすことができるようになっている。空中には動線が持ち上がり、絡み合いながら大屋根を構成し、そのまま屋上のテラスへと連続している。この動線は構造体として機能しており、ガラスのマリオンに等間隔に埋め込まれた柱とともに屋根を支え、巨大な無柱空間を生み出している。この動線を経て空中を散策してゆくと、眼下の地下空間に区分けされたさまざまな種目の競技場を見下ろせる。そして、移動とともに目に入るスポーツの種目が次々と切り替わってゆく。主体育館は地上レベルにも観客席が設けられ、競技の際には地下レベル、地上レベル、空中からのレベルと3つの角度から競技を眺めることが可能になっている。この主体育館は競技場であるばかりでなく、コンサートやライブパフォーマンス、入学式や卒業式など寧波大学のさまざまな行事で活用される多目的アリーナでもある。通常均質な空間で単一の競技が行われる複合体育施設の空間の形式に対して、多様なアクティビティが同時に存在し、それらをさまざまなレベルの視点から眺めることができる多目的アリーナの空間の形式の提示を試みた。地上レベルから空中で錯綜する動線を登ってゆくと屋上テラスへと辿り着くが、この屋上テラスからは寧波大学ののどかなキャンパスを一望することもできる。

This is a competition design proposal for a gymnasium complex at Ningbo University, located east of Ningbo city in Zhejiang province, China. On a site of about 18,000 square meters, it will house the main gymnasium, covering an area of 8,000 square meters, and separate stadiums for a total of 10 types of sports, including basketball, volleyball, karate, yoga, taekwondo, aerobics and gymnastics. The main gymnasium and the stadiums, each of which is individually partitioned, are planned in an underground space divided by a grid; they can be overlooked from the entrance on the first floor. The aerial passageway floating overhead is intertwined to form a large roof, which leads directly to the rooftop terrace. This passageway supports the roof with columns embedded in glass mullions at regular intervals, creating a huge column-less space. As you stroll along the aerial passageway, you can look down on the sectionalized underground stadiums for various sport events and you could see one event after another as you travel. The main gymnasium has spectator's stands on the ground level as well, allowing spectators to watch the games from three different angles: underground, ground and aerial level. The main gymnasium is not only a stadium, but also a multi-purpose arena used for music concerts, live performances, university ceremonies, and other events at Ningbo University. This is a proposal of a spatial form of a multi-purpose arena in which a variety of activities exist simultaneously and can be viewed from various perspectives, in contrast to the usual spatial form of a sports complex, where single competition is held in a homogenous space. From the rooftop terrace where you could reach via a complex aerial passageway, you can enjoy a panoramic view of Ningbo University's idyllic campus.

Netwrok Diagram

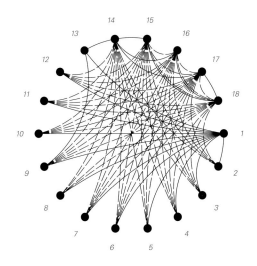

動線の関係
connection of passage

視線の関係
connection of visibility

| 1 | 地下廊下 | underground corridor | 10 | 卓球 | pingpong |
|---|---|---|---|---|---|
| 2 | ヨガ | yoga | 11 | 空手・テコンドー | taekwondo |
| 3 | アスレチック | athletic | 12 | 武術 | bujutsu |
| 4 | バスケットボール | basketball | 13 | 地下回廊 | underground corridor |
| 5 | 主体育館 | main gymnasium | 14 | 地上回廊 | overground corridor |
| 6 | エアロビクス | aerobics | 15 | 空中回廊 | sky corridor |
| 7 | 体操 | gymnastics | 16 | 空中回廊 | sky corridor |
| 8 | バレーボール | volleyball | 17 | 空中回廊 | sky corridor |
| 9 | 階段室 | staircase | 18 | 屋上テラス | roof terrace |

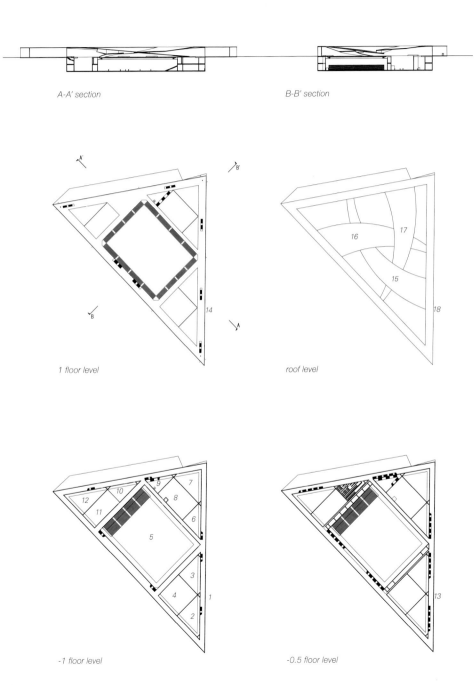

A-A' section

B-B' section

1 floor level

roof level

-1 floor level

-0.5 floor level

# バコロドシュガー ミュージアム
## Bacolod Sugar Museum

*2017- ,Bacolod, Philippines*

## 菱形の単位の 連鎖による層状の空間
*A layered space with a series of rhombic units*

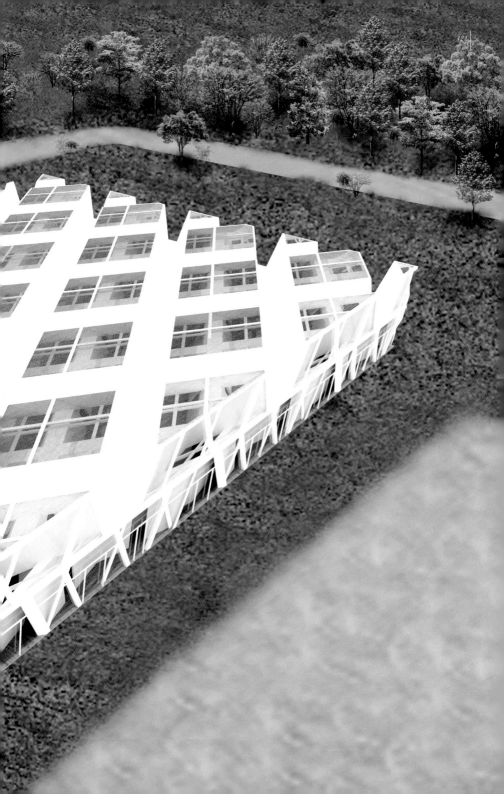

*Three Dimensional Icon*

菱形の単位を
反復させてずらして重ねる
レイヤー状の空間

周期的反復
*repetition*

レイヤー
*layering*

A layered space in which
the rhombic units are repeated
and shifted

フィリピンのネグロス島の中西部のバコロド市の中心に計画された博物館、多目的公共施設である。ネグロス島は砂糖きびのプランテーションを中心とする農業が主要な産業で、この建物は砂糖の製造の過程とネグロス島の歴史と風土について展示を行うミュージアムの計画である。ほかに砂糖をふんだんに使用したケーキを食べることができるカフェ、ラウンジ、現地のお菓子や特産品、バコロドの農作物等を扱うマーケット、市民のための多目的な空間や、バコロドを訪れる人のための観光案内所も併設されている。このような多様なプログラムを納める博物館・美術館・公共建築の形式を、砂糖の結晶を模した菱形の形態の反復操作によってデザインした。建物は1階建てであるが、上下2層となっており、1層目は菱形の幾何学によって生み出された空間が傾斜した壁面によって構成されている。その構成が上下反転した2層目が、1層目と位置をずらしながら重ね合わされることによって、吹き抜けの空間が立体的に交錯しながら重なり合う、多様な連続性と空間的な繋がりを持つ流動的なネットワーク型の空間が生み出されている。この1層目の空間と2層目の空間の間に、照明や空調などの設備用の梁が架け渡されることによって、空間に緊張感が生まれている。同時に、2層目の空間の上部にはトップライトが設けられているが、そのトップライトの梁の交点の位置を中心からずらすことによって、全体的に多様な層状のエレメントがずれながら積層されている空間が生み出されている。訪れる人がそれを知覚することにより層状に視差的にずれた知覚を体験する特異なネットワーク型の空間が生み出されることを期待している。

This is a museum and multipurpose public facility planned in the heart of Bacolod city in the mid-western part of Negros Island, Philippines. This building is planned as a museum to exhibit the process of sugar production and the history and climate of this region as its main industry is agriculture, focused on sugar cane plantation. There will also be a café that offers sugar-laden cakes, a lounge, a market selling local sweets, specialties and Bacolod produced crops, a multi-purpose space for citizens, and a tourist information center for visitors to Bacolod. The design of the museums and public building to house these diverse programs is based on the iterative manipulation of the rhombic form of sugar crystals. This one-story structure building is composed of two layers. The space of the first layer is created by the rhombic geometry with sloping walls. The second layer, which is an inverted version of the first, is superimposed on the first layer while shifting its positions, creating a fluid networked space with various continuities and spatial connections, as the spaces in the atrium overlap and intersect in a three-dimensional manner. Between the first- and second-layer spaces, beams for mechanical equipment such as lighting and air conditioning are placed, creating a sense of tension in the space. At the same time, by shifting the position of the intersection of the beam of the skylight at the top of the second layer of space from the center, an overall space is created in which a variety of layered elements are displaced and stacked. The design is expected to create a unique networked space in which visitors could experience a layered, parallax-shifted perception.

Netwrok Diagram

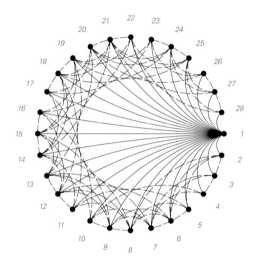

動線の関係
connection of passage

視線の関係
connection of visibility

| 1 | 廊下 | corridor |
|---|---|---|
| 2–4 | カフェ・ラウンジ | cafe lounge |
| 5–13 | 展示室 A | exhibition room A |
| 14–19 | 展示室 B | exhibition room B |
| 20 | トイレ | toilet |
| 21–22 | 多目的室 | multipurpose room |
| 23–25 | マーケット | market |
| 26–28 | 観光案内 | tourism information |

*A-A' section*

*roof level*

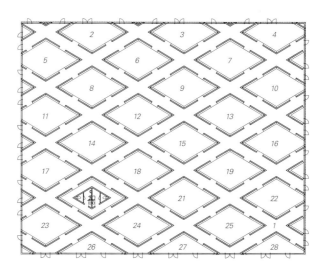

*1 floor level*

# ハシエンダ
# レセプションセンター
## Hacienda Reception Cen

*2016- Bacolod, Philippines*

## 三角形の中で
## 枝分れ編み込まれた空間

*Diverged and interwoven space in a tria*

*Three Dimensional Icon*

編み込まれ、
枝分れと合流を繰り広げる
動線空間

編みこみ
*weave*

枝分かれ
*branch*

Circulation space that is
interwoven and repeats
diversion and convergence

砂糖きび畑が一面に広がるフィリピン・バコロド市の郊外に、民間の不動産開発会社が開発を行っている住宅地のエントランスの脇に建設が予定されている公民館。主に住民のための多目的な空間であるとともに、来訪者のための受付・案内所としての機能も担う。集会室、交流ラウンジ、図書室、スタジオ、キッチンなど住民のための機能のほかに、レセプション、玄関ホール、ゲストルームなどゲストのための機能が収められている。いわば住民が自分の家の部屋だけでまかない切れない機能を収めた第二のホームであると言える。大勢のゲストを招いた際のパーティのための空間や、ゲストのための宿泊施設、図書館、日曜大工や創作のためのスタジオを住民同士で共有しながら活用できる、多目的な第二のリビングルームとしての機能を果たすことが期待されている。そしてその空間は、細長い空間が全体的に三角形の平面を構成するように立体的に編み込まれ、枝分かれをしながら、上昇と下降を繰り返し、その途中のいたる所に吹き溜まりや半屋外のテラスなどの多様な場が生まれる。空間の構成はあたかも迷宮のように複雑で錯綜しているものの、三角形の幾何学によって規則的に反復しているために、一見迷宮のような込み入った構成が、ルールを読み解くことによって、目的の空間へと効率よく辿り着くことができるようになっている。建物のすべての壁面はガラスで構成されており、同時にすべての構成が三角形の幾何学の中で規則的に反復しているために、空間のエレメントは相互に反射し合い、あたかも万華鏡のような無限の広がりを感じさせる特異な空間が生み出されることになる。

In a suburb of Bacolod city, the Philippines, where sugar cane fields cover the majority of the area, this community center is planned to be built beside the entrance of a residential area being developed by a private real estate development company. As mainly a multi-purpose space for residents and serves as a reception and information center for visitors, it houses functions for guests such as a reception area, entrance hall, and a guest room as well as functions for residents such as a meeting room, lounge, library, studio, and kitchen. In a sense, it is a second home that contains functions that cannot be covered by each of the residents' home in such a way that it serves as a versatile second living room where residents share the space for large parties, lodging for guests, a library, and a studio for DIYs and creative work. The space is knitted in three dimensions so that the long and narrow spaces form a triangular plane as a whole, while it branches out, repeats ups and downs, and creates diverse places such as congestion space and semi-outdoor terraces along the way. Despite the complexity of the labyrinthine spatial structure, the geometry of the triangle allows for regular repetition, so that what appears to be a labyrinthine structure can be effectively traced to its destination by decoding the rules. Composed mostly of glass, all walls of the building recur regularly among the geometry of a triangle, and therefore the elements of the space reflect each other and create a unique space that gives the impression of a kaleidoscopic, infinite expanse.

Netwrok Diagram

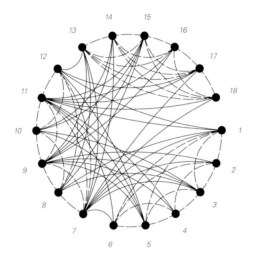

動線の関係
connection of passage

視線の関係
connection of visibility

| | | | | | | | |
|---|---|---|---|---|---|---|---|
| 1 | 玄関ホール | entrance hall | | 10 | 集会室 | meeting room |
| 2 | スタジオ | studio | | 11 | 交流ラウンジ | lounge |
| 3 | 浴室・トイレ | bath and toilet | | 12 | 集会室 | meeting room |
| 4 | 図書室 | library | | 13 | 屋上テラス | roof terrace |
| 5 | キッチン | kitchen | | 14 | 屋上テラス | roof terrace |
| 6 | ゲストルーム | guest room | | 15 | 屋上テラス | roof terrace |
| 7 | 交流ラウンジ | lounge | | 16 | 屋上テラス | roof terrace |
| 8 | 集会室 | meeting room | | 17 | 屋上テラス | roof terrace |
| 9 | 交流ラウンジ | lounge | | 18 | 屋上テラス | roof terrace |

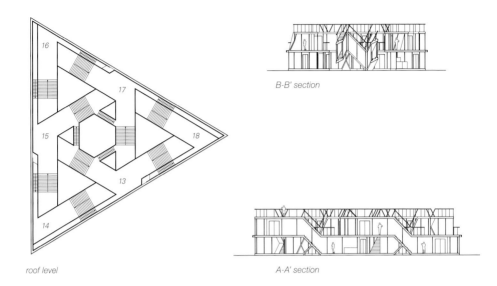

roof level

B-B' section

A-A' section

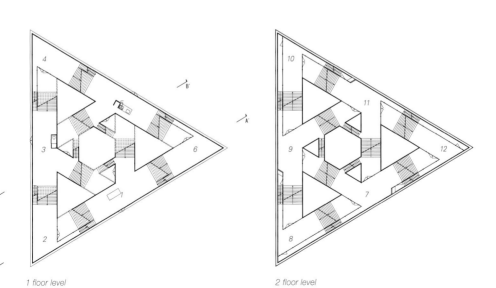

1 floor level

2 floor level

# ランジット・マックーニ・ミュージアム

## Ranjit Makkuni Museum

2015– New Delhi, India

## 枝分れ捻じれ反転し重ね合わされた空間

### Diverged, twisted, inverted and superimposed space

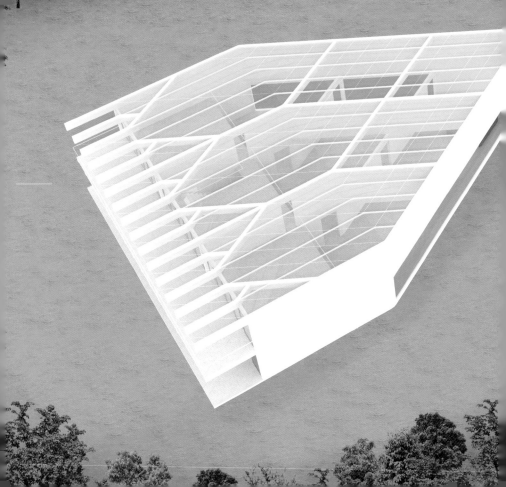

枝分かれ
*branch*

*Three Dimensional Icon*

枝分れを繰り広げる
壁面による空間がねじれ
反転し重ね合わされる

レイヤー
*layering*

The space created by the
diverging wall surface that
is twisted, inverted and
superimposed

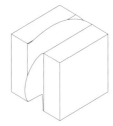
ツイスト
*twist*

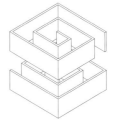
反転
*reverse*

このプロジェクトはインドを代表するアーティスト、ランジット・マックーニのために計画された美術館兼住宅である。マックーニは、さまざまな表現をコンピュータ・ジェネレイテッドな映像や音楽、デジタルデバイスを駆使して展開するメディア・アーティストである。一方、作曲、演奏を手掛ける音楽家であり、同時にインド国内でさまざまな美術館や博物館のプロデュースも行っているマルチ・クリエーターでもある。本プロジェクトはマックーニ自身の作品を収蔵し、一般に公開するための美術展示室とアトリエ、事務所、アーティスト本人が生活するための住宅の機能を複合している。建物はパブリックな機能が配された東ウィングとプライベートな機能が配された西ウィングという東西二つのウィングから構成されている。東ウィングの1階が一般の人が来訪可能な美術展示室、図書室となっており、2階にはアトリエと事務室が収まる。西ウィングの1階にはリビングルームやキッチン、ダイニング、水回りが収められ、2階にはマスターベッドルームとゲストベッドルームが設けられている。これらを束ねるのが枝分かれした空間の構成であり、2層に分かれた壁が枝分かれを繰り広げ、その二つの層が建物中央部分で捻れながら上下が反転し、重ね合わされるという論理によって、立体的で複雑なネットワーク型の空間が生み出されている。単純な枝分かれの論理が立体的に錯綜することによって、シンプルな論理に基づく構成でありながら複雑で多様な空間が生み出されている。多様な見えがかりに溢れたネットワーク型の空間の論理によって美術展示室や生活の空間が生み出されることより、訪れる人々や居住するクライアントにとって日々の生活が発見に満ちたものになることを期待している。

The project is a museum and dwelling space designed for the iconic Indian artist, Ranjit Makkuni, a media artist who uses computer-generated imagery, music and digital devices in his various forms of expression. At the same time, he is a musician who composes and performs music as well as a multi-creator who coordinates various museums and art galleries in India. This building functions as an art gallery for collecting and exhibiting Makkuni's works, a studio, an office, and his own residence. The building consists of two wings: East Wing is for public and West Wing is for private space. The first floor of the East Wing houses the art gallery and library, while the studio and office are located on the second floor. The ground floor of the West Wing houses the living room, kitchen, dining and wet area, while the master bedroom and guest bedroom are located on the second floor. What binds them together is the composition of the diverging space—the logic of the two layers of walls branching out and twisting in the center of the building, reversing up and down and superimposing themselves, that creates a three-dimensional, complex network of spaces. Because of the three-dimensional complexity of simple diverging logic, a complex and diverse space is created even though the composition is based on simple logic. By creating art galleries and living spaces based on the logic of a networked space full of complicated visible outlines, our goal is to make daily life full of discoveries for the visitors and the clients who would live there.

Netwrok Diagram

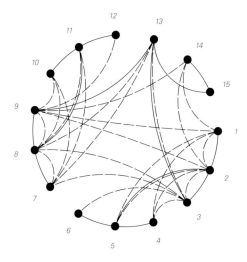

動線の関係
connection of passage

視線の関係
connection of visibility

| | | | | | |
|---|---|---|---|---|---|
| 1 | 図書室 | library | 9 | リビングルーム | living room |
| 2 | 展示室 1 | exhibition room 1 | 10 | ベッドルーム | bedroom |
| 3 | 展示室 2 | exhibition room 2 | 11 | 階段ホール | staircase |
| 4 | スタジオ | studio | 12 | ゲストルーム | guest room |
| 5 | 階段ホール | staircase | 13 | 外庭 | public garden |
| 6 | オフィス | office | 14 | 内庭 | private garden |
| 7 | 浴室・トイレ | bath and toilet | 15 | 中庭 | patio |
| 8 | キッチン・食堂 | kitchen | | | |

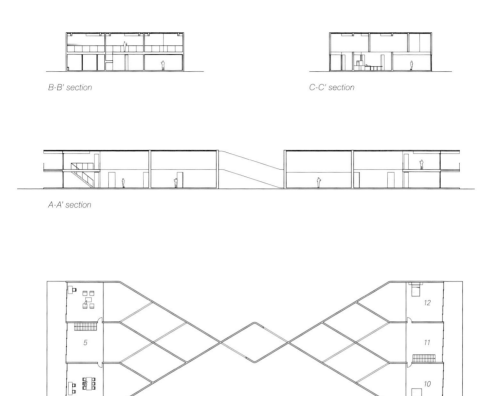

*B-B' section*

*C-C' section*

*A-A' section*

*2 floor level*

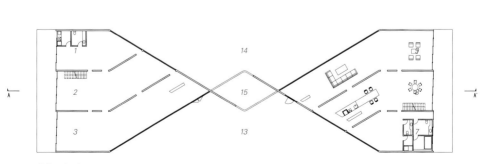

*1 floor level*

# フォトクレジット

photo credit

鳥村鋼一　*koichi torimura*
　*p044-059*（villa kanousan）、*p074-091*（s-house）

木奥恵三　*keizo kioku*
　*p062-063*（中心が移動し続ける都市）（提供：NTT Inter Communication Center [ICC]）

「中心が移動し続ける都市」（*p062-063*）は松山剛士 *Takashi Matsuyama* との協同による。

# 柄沢祐輔

Yuusuke Karasawa

1976年東京都生まれ。建築家、柄沢祐輔建築設計事務所主宰。慶應義塾大学大学院政策・メディア研究科建築・都市デザインコース修了。文化庁派遣芸術家在外研修制度にてMVRDV（オランダ）在籍、坂茂建築設計勤務を経て、2006年に柄沢祐輔建築設計事務所設立。『10+1』48号「アルゴリズム的思考と建築」特集（INAX出版、2007年）では責任編集を務めるなど、情報論的、あるいはアルゴリズム的な思考を軸とした建築・都市空間の探求を行なっている。2011年英国D&AD賞SpatialDesign部門受賞。主な展覧会に「日本の家1945年以降の建築と暮し」（MAXXI国立21世紀美術館、バービカン・センター、東京国立近代美術館、2016-2017）、「Japan-ness. Architecture and urbanism in Japan since 1945」（ポンピドゥー・センター・メス、2017-2018）など。s-houseの模型はフランス国立ポンピドゥー・センターの所蔵コレクションとして収蔵されている。

Born in Tokyo in 1976. Architect, and President of Yuusuke Karasawa Architects. Graduated with an MA in Architecture and Urban Design from Keio University in 2001. Worked at MVRDV as a trainee under the Japanese Government Overseas Study Program for Artist from 2002 to 2003, and after working at Shigeru Ban Architects from 2004 to 2005, established Yuusuke Karasawa Architects in 2006. He explores architecture and urban space created by algorithmic method and thinking. He was the chief editor of the special issue "Algorithmic thinking and architecture" on "10+1" magazine vol.48 (INAX publishing, 2007). He won D&AD Awards (England) Spatial Design Category in 2011. His works have been presented in major exhibitions including, among others, "The Japanese House: Architecture and Life after 1945" (MAXXI: National Museum of 21st Century Arts, Barbican Centre, The National Museum of Modern Art, Tokyo 2016-2017), and "Japan-ness. Architecture and urbanism in Japan since 1945" (Centre Pompidou-Metz 2017-2018). The model of "s-house" is stored in Centre Pompidou's collection.

現代建築家コンセプト・シリーズ 28

柄沢祐輔　アルゴリズムによるネットワーク型の建築をめざして

| 発 行 日 | 2021年1月25日 第1刷発行 |
|---|---|
| 著 者 | 柄沢祐輔 |
| 発 行 者 | ジン・ソン・モンテサーノ |
| 発 行 所 | LIXIL出版<br>〒136-8535 東京都江東区大島 2-1-1<br>TEL.03-3638-8021　FAX.03-3638-8022<br>www.livingculture.lixil/publish |
| 編 集 | 髙木伸哉 (flick studio) |
| 翻 訳 | 今泉敦子 (p022-025)、フレーズクレーズ (p004-008, p026-161解説文) |
| デ ザ イ ン | 浅田農 (MATCH and Company Co., Ltd.) |
| 制 作 協 力 | 田口陽子 |
| 印刷・製本 | 株式会社加藤文明社 |

ISBN 978-4-86480-050-1 C0352